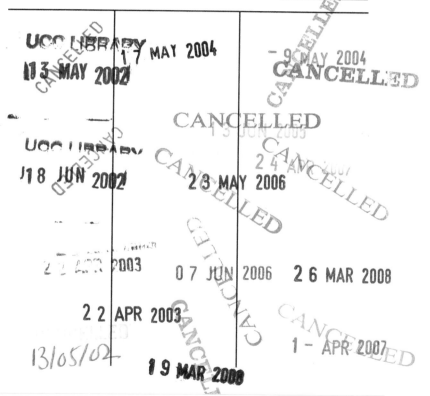

FOUNDATIONS OF BUSINESS ECONOMICS

Much of the literature for business economics courses has tended to be highly technical and theoretical. *Foundations of Business Economics* redresses this imbalance by focusing on real-life business situations.

The book provides a readable explanation of microeconomic analysis in terms of real business practice. The author looks at the various issues involved, including: the economic way of thinking; the business environment; product markets; factor markets; and general equilibrium. The underlying theme is the way in which markets link together interdependent economic activities, so the discussion begins in an individual bookshop and ends with general equilibrium models of the entire economic system. On the way, attention is paid to markets facing and resolving problems of information.

The book is largely free of mathematics and technical detail and is therefore easily accessible. It will be particularly valuable to those students who are primarily interested in the human side of industry and economic specialists feeling the need to come down to earth from the austere heights of pure theory.

Harry Townsend is Emeritus Professor of Economics at Lancaster University. He helped organise the Edwards Seminars in Industrial Administration and has played a key role in establishing business economics as a subject.

FOUNDATIONS OF BUSINESS ECONOMICS

Markets and Prices

Harry Townsend

ROUTLEDGE

London and New York

First published 1995
by Routledge
11 New Fetter Lane, London EC4P 4EE

Simultaneously published in the USA and Canada
by Routledge
29 West 35th Street, New York, NY 10001

Typeset in Garamond by LaserScript, Mitcham, Surrey
Printed and bound in Great Britain by
Mackays of Chatham PLC, Chatham, Kent

British Library Cataloguing in Publication Data
A catalogue record for this book is available from the British Library

Library of Congress Cataloging in Publication Data
A catalogue record for this book has been requested

ISBN 0–415–12073–x (hbk)
ISBN 0–415–12074–8 (pbk)

CONTENTS

Part III Product markets

Part IV Factor markets

Part V Conclusion

FIGURES

TABLES

PREFACE

Not so long ago 'business studies' was a succinct definition of economics, bettering Alfred Marshall – 'political economy or economics is a study of mankind in the ordinary business of life; it examines that part of individual and social action which is most closely connected with the attainment and with the use of the material requisites of wellbeing' – by some forty words. Nowadays, economists have widened their gaze to take in all spheres of choice, and business studies has grown to encompass accounting, business finance, business history, commercial law, industrial organisation, information technology, labour relations, marketing, operational research, social psychology, statistics, and systems analysis along with some economics. In different permutations and combinations these subjects make up the syllabi of degrees in business administration, management science and managerial economics which are remarkable for breadth and depth of intellectual challenge.

Economics has a special role in such degrees. It provides integrating analysis of business environments and business behaviour that links together the other subjects into coherent courses of study. Such integration is the aim of this book addressed to second-year students feeling the need to see how their studies fit together and especially feeling the need not simply to learn economic theory but also to see how it applies to the business world.

This has dictated the approach, explaining economic analysis so far as possible in terms of real business situations: pure competition in terms of taxicabs, efficient markets in terms of the turf, cartels in terms of OPEC, market failure in terms of advertising and pollution, and so on. Mathematics has been kept to a minimum.

This may seem odd as many business students are decidedly numerate and many business subjects are distinctly mathematical. However, there are also students whose interests lie on the human side of industry in business history, labour relations, law, marketing and social psychology.

I am conscious that I owe a lot to others for many topics discussed. Chapter 1's starting point in the second-hand book trade brings to mind many shops introduced by Sir Kenneth Alexander and his discussions of second-hand trading whilst conducting a tour of Scottish tinkers' yards. Chapter 2 reflects the fact that I was once tutee and research assistant to R.H. Coase. An early version of Chapter 3 was written in collaboration with Sir Ronald Edwards before his untimely death. I was introduced to the economics of taxicabs by Sir Roy Allen and Ralph Turvey. Three oil companies taught me most of what I know about the oil trade, two of them having the politeness to pay consulting fees whilst doing so. I hope that full acknowledgement to articles and books is made in the relevant chapters.

Many friends have commented on the manuscript. Especial thanks are due to Roger Inman, of Harrison Fisher & Taylor Eye-witness Cutlery, who brought his common sense and tact to bear on the entire book. I am also indebted to my colleagues at Lancaster, particularly Harvey Armstrong, Paul Ferguson, Alasdair Macbean and Bob Rothschild. They should not be found guilty by association.

I am grateful to Lord Bauer, B.S. Yamey, the Consumers' Association, and the Open University for permission to incorporate copyright material.

Thanks are also due to Audrey Bamber for careful and sensitive copy-editing, and to the Economics Department for secretarial help in the days before I took to DIY word-processing.

HARRY TOWNSEND
Department of Economics
The Management School
University of Lancaster

Part I

INTRODUCTION

1

THE ECONOMIC WAY OF THINKING

1 INTRODUCTION

The Economist Bookshop, the biggest London shop specialising in social and political sciences, was for many years jointly owned by *The Economist* newspaper and the London School of Economics (LSE). Its board of directors were therefore not short of economic expertise. The Academic Board of LSE objected to the way second-hand books were confined to a narrow set of shelves at the back of the shop, arguing that the second-hand trade should be expanded, mainly for the benefit of students with limited means but also for the profitability of the shop as a whole. The manageress, a very determined lady, was not impressed. She claimed that second-hand books reduced sales of new books. Who was right?

Common sense and fixed quantities

Common sense is on the side of the manageress. Second-hand books are substitutes for new ones, and the more you sell of the first the less you will sell of the other: students take so many courses per year and need so many books, no more and no less. This idea that we need readily countable quantities of goods, so many books per year, and in the wider world, so many tons of wheat, yards of cloth, barrels of oil and so on, is widely held. It lies behind arguments that home suppliers are bound to suffer from foreign competition, that the way to cure unemployment is to share a fixed quantity of work, that what is good for one must be bad for another. It is quite foreign to the economic way of thinking.

Systematic relationships between variables

Quantities of goods bought and sold are not fixed in amount but variables, quantities that vary in a systematic way with changes in underlying determinants. Thus members of the Academic Board advocating expansion of second-hand sales urged, first, that the quantity of new books sold per year varies with the price of new books, the lower the price the greater the quantity sold. The possibility of reselling books after use reduces the effective price of a new book. If a book costing £12 new could be resold second-hand after one year for £4, its use for one year would cost £8 instead of £12. At an effective price of £8 a greater number of new books would be purchased.

Secondly, they argued that this relationship between the effective price of new books and the numbers sold would be affected by a number of surrounding circumstances. In particular, the number bought at any price would be smaller the cheaper the available substitutes. Second-hand books are substitutes for new ones, so an increase in the supply of second-hand books would of itself reduce the quantity of new books purchased at any price. They argued that the extension of sales of new books consequent on the reduction in effective price (in our example, from £12 to £8) would more than offset the fall in quantities of new books sold at any price (£12, £8 or whatever).

Economic arguments depend upon theory and fact. The answer to the bookshop's problem evidently depends upon the strength of the two relationships of, first, quantities bought at alternative prices and, secondly, quantities bought and the availability of substitutes. This is typical of the economic way of thinking. It specifies the relationships to consider, particular outcomes depending upon the magnitudes involved. The facts have to be established in each particular case. Economic theory shows what facts to look for.

This way of thinking is an improvement on common sense which easily mistakes surface appearance for insight. In the case of the bookshop, premises were continuously extended and additional space provided for both new and second-hand books. Sales of new books expanded along with sales of second-hand books. This does not prove that second-hand sales are good for the new-book trade: even more new books might have been sold if second-hand books had not been available; but the historical record provides no refutation.[1]

Careful account of the possibilities of substitution lies behind a good deal of economic analysis. Section 2 considers the possibility of substituting one input for another in the production of a single product. Section 3 is devoted to the substitution of one product for another by changing the disposition of factors of production. Increasing production of one good at the expense of another leads to the concept of economic cost being opportunity cost, the cost of one line of action being the value of the most desirable alternative forgone. Section 4 is devoted to opportunity cost, and Section 5 to the ways in which opportunity cost may differ from accounting cost.

2 SUBSTITUTING INPUTS IN PRODUCTION

Cud-chewing cattle have a simple digestive system that is able to extract or synthesise all nutrients needed from a diet of starch, protein and roughage.[2] The daily requirements of a 500 kg bullock growing at a rate of 0.5 kg per day has been estimated to be 4.0 kg of starch equivalent (SE), 0.5 kg of protein equivalent (PE), and 0.5 kg fibre. These may be provided by a variety of feedstuffs; but suppose, for simplicity, that there are only two possibilities, dried grass and barley. The percentages of starch, protein and fibre in dried grass and barley are roughly:

	SE (%)	PE (%)	Fibre (%)
dried grass meal	50	10	20
barley	70	7	5

8 kg of dried grass, 5.7 kg of barley or some proportionate combination of the two would therefore supply all the starch required; 5 kg of dried grass, 7.1 kg of barley or some proportionate combination would supply the protein; and 2.5 kg of dried grass, 10 kg of barley or some proportionate combination would supply the fibre. Combinations of dried grass and barley which would be sufficient for all nutrients are depicted in Figure 1.1.

Combinations of grass and barley on or to the right of AB would provide sufficient starch; combinations on or to the right of CD would provide sufficient protein; and combinations on or to the right of EF would provide sufficient fibre. The segmented curve AGHF shows the smallest amounts of dried grass that may be combined with increasing amounts of barley, or vice versa, the

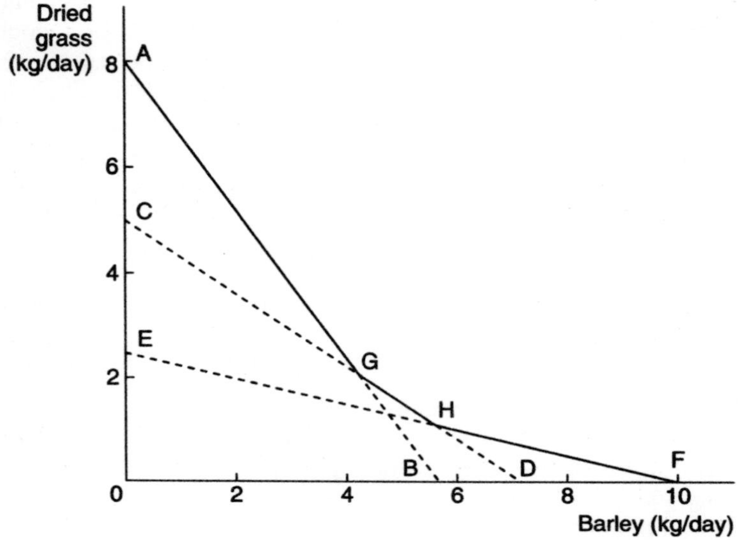

Figure 1.1 Feeding bullocks

smallest amounts of barley that may be combined with increasing amounts of dried grass, whilst maintaining an adequate diet. Curves such as AGHF which show alternative ways of producing a given level of product are termed equal-product curves, or isoquants. AGHF is an isoquant for producing 0.5 kg liveweight beef per day with one bullock. Providing we add a bullock each time, the isoquant for 1 kg beef per day would be twice the distance from the origin, starting at 16 kg dried grass and ending at 20 kg barley; the isoquant for 1.5 kg beef would be three times as far from the origin, and so on. A set of isoquants, or isoquant map, provides a means of depicting the technological possibilities.

Between A and G, 1 kg of barley may be substituted for 1.4 kg of dried grass. If substitution is continued beyond G, a kilogram of barley will only replace 0.7 kg of grass because the lower protein content of barley becomes critical. The rate of substitution of 1 kg barley for 0.7 grass continues until H is reached. Between H and F, 1 kg of barley is only sufficient to offset the loss of 0.25 kg of grass because barley is such a poor provider of fibre. The marginal rate of substitution of barley for grass thus diminishes along the isoquant.

This is a general property of isoquants reflecting the imperfect substitutability of different inputs for one another.

Isoquants show that technology alone is not sufficient to decide the least-cost method of production. There are almost always a large number of technological possibilities and choosing between them depends upon the prices of inputs. If dried grass sold for 12p per kilo and barley for 10p, producing beef using only dried grass (as at A) would cost 96p per 0.5 kg of beef, using the combination of inputs at G would cost 67p, at H 69p, and at F 100p. The least-cost method of producing beef would be to feed the combination shown at G.

Combinations of inputs as at G are said to be efficient. Efficiency is defined, following Vilfredo Pareto, as a situation where it is impossible to make any change that would make someone better-off without making anyone worse-off. Isoquants draw attention to two sources of inefficiency in production. It is easy to waste inputs. In our example this would be shown as producing 0.5 kg of beef with a combination of grass and barley lying to the right of AGHF. This is termed technological inefficiency, or 'X-inefficiency', and is shown by the range of costs experienced by firms using similar methods of production. Secondly, a firm may avoid technological inefficiency by choosing inputs located on an isoquant, but choose the wrong combination, such as H instead of G. This is termed 'economic inefficiency'.

Grass and barley may be used to produce things other than beef. The barley, for instance, might be malted. However, these inputs will not be pursued further. Instead, the possibilities of substituting one product for another are examined in terms of ice-cream.

3 SUBSTITUTING ONE PRODUCT FOR ANOTHER

Consider an ice-cream parlour that has daily supplies of 60 kg milk, 51 kg ice-cream powder, and 30 kg sugar, which may be converted into soft ice-cream or conventional ice-cream. Recipes for making 1 kg of each type are as follows:

Soft ice-cream	*Conventional ice-cream*
0.6 kg milk	0.3 kg milk
0.15 kg ice-cream powder	0.5 kg ice-cream powder
0.25 kg sugar	0.2 kg sugar

If all the milk is used for soft ice-cream, there is enough for 100 kg. If it is all used for conventional ice-cream, there is enough for 200 kg; or milk may be shared between the two types, each reduction of 1 kg soft ice-cream releasing sufficient milk for 2 kg conventional ice-cream.

So far as ice-cream powder is concerned, there is enough for 340 kg soft, 102 kg conventional or some combination of the two. For instance, if powder needed for 100 kg soft – 15 kg powder – is released for conventional ice-cream it is sufficient for 30 kg conventional, and, so far as powder is concerned, a possible combination is 240 kg soft plus 30 kg conventional.

There is still need to take account of the third ingredient, sugar. Enough sugar is provided for 120 kg soft or 150 kg conventional, or for some combination of the two. Reducing production of soft ice-cream by 4 kg releases enough sugar to make 5 kg conventional.

Looking at each ingredient successively, however, does not give a full picture of the production possibilities because each type of ice-cream requires all three ingredients. The full picture is provided by Figure 1.2. The limit to output imposed by the supply of milk is shown by the dotted line AB; so far as milk is concerned it is possible to have 100 kg soft and no conventional (A), 200 kg conventional and no soft as at B, or any of the combinations along AB. Similarly, the limit imposed by the powder constraint is shown by CD, and that imposed by the sugar constraint by EF. When account is taken of all three ingredients at the same time, we are left with the area bounded by the origin and the three constraints OAGHD. Any combination of soft and conventional ice-cream falling within this area is attainable, and the maximum amount of conventional that can be produced together with a given amount of soft, and vice versa, is shown by the curve AGHD.

Starting at A, where only soft ice-cream is produced, it may be seen that switching ingredients from soft to conventional provides a relatively large amount of conventional ice-cream, 2 kg, for every kilogram of soft given up. This is because at A there is surplus sugar and powder, and the only ingredient being fully used, milk, is especially suited to conventional ice-cream. As substitution proceeds, G is reached. At this point all the milk and sugar are being employed to make the two products, and additional kilograms of conventional ice-cream can be obtained only by reducing output of soft sufficiently to release the required sugar.

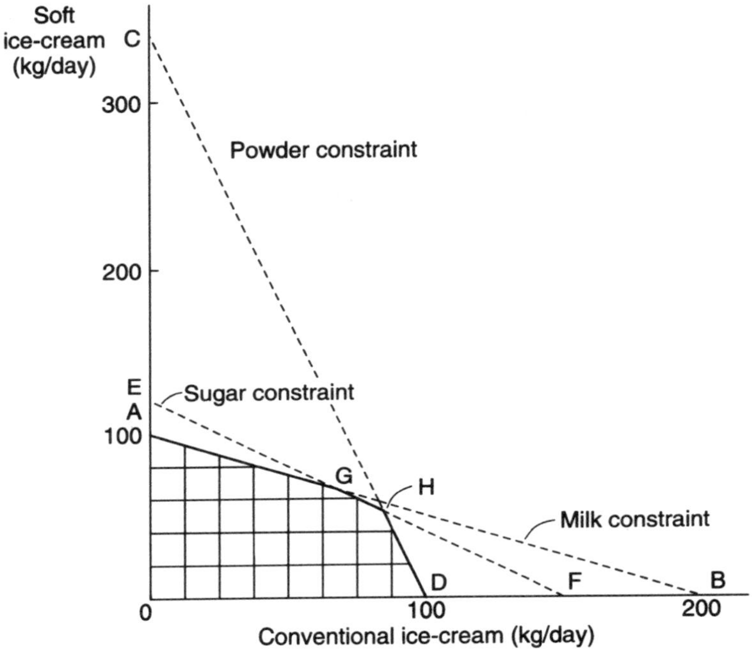

Figure 1.2 Substituting products

Conventional ice-cream needs less sugar than soft, so it is still possible to obtain 1.25 kg of conventional for every kilogram of soft given up. If substitution is carried beyond H, conditions are least favourable for substituting conventional for soft. Combinations of the two products are limited by the available powder, and reducing output of soft by 1 kg releases only 0.15 kg powder, sufficient for 0.3 kg conventional ice-cream. AGHD illustrates the diminishing rate of transformation of one product into another as substitution proceeds.

The frontier AGHD, showing maximum combinations of the two products that may be made with limited resources, is known as a production possibility or transformation curve. Transformation curves are typically convex upwards for the reason that explains the shape of the ice-cream curve. When substitution of one product for another begins it is possible to make use of inputs specially suited to the new product, but as substitution continues favourable conditions are exhausted.

Transformation curves illustrate two further sources of inefficiency. Choice of product combinations lying within the boundary represents technological inefficiency because it would be possible to produce more of one product without reducing the output of the other, or to increase output of both, by moving out to the boundary. Economic efficiency demands in addition that the point on the boundary be chosen that best satisfies consumer demands.

The diminishing rate of transformation of one product into another implies increasing cost of one product in terms of the other. In the ice-cream example, starting from A, a kilogram of conventional ice-cream at first only costs 0.5 kg of soft, after G 0.8 kg of soft must be given up, and beyond H 3.3 kg. The concept of cost as alternative forgone, brings us to opportunity cost.

4 OPPORTUNITY COST

An economic decision involves answering the question 'what difference will it make?', which breaks into two parts: 'what will be the benefit?' and 'what must be given up to gain the benefit?' What has to be given up, the most valuable alternative forgone, is the opportunity cost. There are usually lots of alternatives to any course under consideration, and the best of these alternatives is the relevant opportunity to take into account. The value of this best opportunity forgone is the opportunity cost of the decision.

Since one cannot give up an opportunity that is already past, opportunity cost is by its very nature forward looking, and, as it depends upon appraisals of the future, it is subjective. This does not mean that it is arbitrary, that reasonable men cannot agree on its estimation or agree on the way estimates will change as unexpected events unfold. It does mean, however, that past accounts only indicate opportunity cost in special circumstances.

Opportunity cost and personal decisions

The cost of reading this book is not the price that must have been paid by reader or library. The best disposition of that payment was a cost sometime in the past, but it is over and done with. Now the cost of reading is the value of the best alternative use of time.

If this reading is part of higher education, it should be clear that the cost of such education is not simply a sum of money payments related to term time. Food is necessary whether a student is at university or not, and so the cost of victuals form no part of the cost of education. On the other hand, if time were not devoted to study it might be used for earning a living. Hence, a large component in the cost of university education is income forgone by students.

This component evidently varies between individuals. The average earnings of young women exceed those of young men, and so the cost of female education is on average greater than that of male education. Older people in general earn more than younger and so the cost of education to a mature student is usually greater than to an adolescent. The greater the possible earnings of an individual the greater the cost of his education: the two years Mick Jagger, of the Rolling Stones, spent at LSE must have been amongst the most costly ever. As average earnings rise with increasing productivity so does the opportunity cost of education, and a one-sided case has been made out on these lines for reducing the duration of courses.[3]

There is such a thing as a free lunch

Austere economists are fond of quoting Phineas T. Barnum's dictum that 'there is no such thing as a free lunch'. Like most folk wisdom this is not always true. If men and women are left unemployed their labour is lost forever. The cost of man-hours unused is whatever value, possibly negative, that is placed on enforced leisure: it is not the wage that would be paid with employment. One of the exasperating consequences of failure to recognise the nature of opportunity cost is the persistence of politicians arguing that projects which would provide work for the unemployed cannot be afforded because the cost would be too high. The opportunity cost of employing a man without work is near zero, whilst the cost of leaving him unemployed is the value of the output he would otherwise produce.

A less portentous example of zero opportunity cost is the use of an existing facility. In the absence of congestion the opportunity cost of an additional vehicle crossing a bridge is zero, and so most toll-bridges require some other justification than the need to recoup 'the cost of the bridge'. Similar considerations apply to uncongested art galleries, museums and public parks.

Varying opportunity cost

Capacity on commuter lines is governed by the number of travellers at peak times and is available off-peak whether it is used or not: beyond additional wear and tear on plant there is no capital cost of its off-peak use. Similar situations arise in seasonal trades such as hotels, theatres, airlines, buses and coaches, telecommunications, gas, oil and electricity. The cost of supplying electricity off-peak is made up almost entirely of energy cost, the cost of coal, oil or nuclear fuel burned to generate electricity. This is low off-peak because only the most fuel-efficient power stations are kept on stream. Hence, the justification of low off-peak tariffs when charges are based on what the electricity costs.

Failure to recognise the nature of economic cost lay behind the retrograde decision to require Her Majesty's Stationery Office (HMSO) to charge 'commercial' prices for official publications instead of following the former practice of charging a standard price per page to cover printing and binding. The cost of an official publication to a member of the public is not a pro rata share of the total outlay by HMSO. When official publications have to be produced for the needs of Ministries and Parliament, the setup costs have to be incurred whether the public buys or not and so the bulk of publication costs cannot be attributed to the general public. The present practice has led to such grotesqueries as the monopolistic pricing of Monopolies Commission reports.

Opportunity cost is of such fundamental importance that one might expect estimates of opportunity costs to be the most readily available cost figures. Management accountants indeed are aware of their importance and make special efforts to provide data for estimating opportunity costs. However, financial and cost accountants usually have different purposes in mind and have strong attachment to the accounting conventions observed in their duties of stewardship.

A prime duty of financial accountants is to keep track of money flows to make sure that no funds are diverted dishonestly. This duty leads to emphasis on payments rather than costs, and on the need to recover past outlays on materials, components, plant and machinery so that money is not taken out of a business when it is needed to keep the money value of capital intact. Such attitudes of mind carry over from financial to cost accountants seeking to record costs incurred. There is therefore plenty of room for confusion over accounting and economic concepts of costs.

5 ECONOMIC COST AND ACCOUNTING COST

The differing approaches of economists and accountants may be seen in a simple example. Consider a manufacturer of electrical cable. Copper rod is extruded to form thin wires that are twisted together, covered with plastic, and assembled into two-core and three-core before receiving a final insulation. How might an accountant and economist calculate the cost of producing 100,000 metres of domestic flex per week? There are costs of materials, labour and management, machinery and factory space to take into account.

Materials

If materials are bought in specially, accountant and economist will agree that the cost of the materials is the amount of money spent on them: from the economist's point of view, the money represents the possibility of the next most valued alternative. An accountant will probably give the same kind of answer if materials are taken from stock, the cost to him is what has been paid. An economist will give different answers depending on the alternatives open to management. One possibility is to sell the materials to outside firms, which gives a material cost equal to resale receipts less the costs of arranging and carrying out such a sale. This possibility is only likely to be relevant if purchases of stocks have been exceptionally lucky or unlucky, and if it is ignored in these circumstances costs will be underestimated or overestimated. In most cases transaction costs inhibit resale of stocks. A second possibility is to use the materials for some other product, in which case the cost of materials is the contribution to profits that the materials would make in the other use. From an economic point of view costs and revenues cannot be kept in separate categories.

Wages and salaries

Treatment of wages and salaries does not differ much between accountants and economists. To the accountant they are simply the product of numbers employed and wage or salary rates. In the case of sole-proprietorships and partnerships, the accountant does not regard the work of proprietor or partner as giving rise to a cost, whereas an economist considers the highest earnings they could earn in alternative employment to be a cost to the business. In addition an economist will deduct wages and salaries for periods of notice agreed for weekly-paid and salaried staff plus redundancy payment entitlements, because these would have to be paid whether people worked or not.

Capital costs

Further differences arise with capital costs. Accountants do not regard interest on owners' capital (whether ordinary shareholders, partners or proprietors) as a cost, whereas to economists the owners are regarded as forgoing the return on investment elsewhere at similar risk and so return on owners' capital is a cost. This may be of considerable importance when deciding in monopoly cases whether excessive profits are being earned. In addition there are differences in the treatment of depreciation.

Accountants regard depreciation as a fraction of original cost, or original cost adjusted to allow for inflation, to be recovered each year of a machine's life, the fraction depending upon the method employed (such as straight-line, which deducts equal amounts each year, or decreasing balance, which deducts equal percentages each year). Economists believe, with Omar Khayýam, that 'the moving finger writes, and having writ, moves on: nor all your piety nor wit shall lure it back to cancel half a line'. Bygones are forever bygones, and the original cost of a machine is quite irrelevant. The cost of a machine depends upon the alternatives available. It could be the earnings that could be made in some other line of production, interest on the resale value net of transaction costs, interest on the scrap value, or economic depreciation.

From an economic point of view depreciation is the fall in the value of an asset over a period of time. The present value of the future net receipts from its use may be estimated for the beginning of a period and for the end of a period: the difference between these two estimates is economic depreciation. An asset may fall in value because of the passage of time or because it is used more intensively. Intensive use may increase depreciation, not because it reduces the time available to recover payment for the machine but because it involves sacrifice of net receipts in the future. This element of depreciation is known as 'user cost'. It is clear that economic depreciation is not given objectively but is a matter of expectations about the future.

Differences between accounting cost and economic cost are summarised in Table 1.1.

Common costs

Another area where economists and accountants differ is in the allocation of common costs. Accountants allocate all costs between the activities being pursued together. If the activities are simply undertaken alongside one another there is no disagreement; but where there are items common to two or more activities economists argue that there is no logical basis for splitting the cost of these items.

Take the case of a research manager deciding whether to undertake two projects, A and B. The cost of A on its own is £700,000, and of B on its own £600,000. If the two projects are undertaken together, the total cost is £1,200,000 giving a saving of £100,000. Now consider the allocation of costs between A and B. If A were to be chosen on its own, the cost would be £700,000

Table 1.1 Accounting cost and economic cost

Item	*Accounting cost*	*Economic cost*
Materials	Quantity × price	If special purchase: quantity × price. From stock: resale price minus transaction costs, or net revenue in other product.
Workers	Employment × wage	Employment × wage minus notice and redundancy entitlements.
Staff	Employment × salary	As workers but with longer period of notice.
Owner-manager	Zero	Income forgone in best alternative occupation.
Plant and machinery	If owned: depreciation on original or inflation adjusted cost. If financed by borrowing: interest plus depreciation.	Interest and return for risk plus depreciation as loss in present value of future net receipts, or earnings in some other line, or interest on resale value net of transaction costs, or interest on scrap value.

instead of £1,200,000 and so the difference made by including B is £500,000. Similarly, if B were chosen on its own, the cost would be £600,000 instead of £1,200,000 and so the difference made by including A is £600,000. It is therefore possible to allocate £1,100,000 between the two projects, but there remains a common cost of £100,000 which can only be attributed to the two projects together.

Accountants have many conventions for distributing common costs but they are all arbitrary and may be misleading. Suppose that A would contribute £690,000 to net revenue, and B £540,000: together they would contribute £1,300,000. If the common cost were split equally between the two projects, the cost of B, at £550,000, would appear to exceed its contribution and so, presumably it should not be undertaken. The cost of A on its own would then exceed its net revenue and so, presumably, should not be undertaken either. Common costs, as their name implies, have to be considered in common. Nothing is gained by allocating such costs. Providing A and B both cover their attributable costs and together provide revenue in excess of total cost they are worth pursuing together.

6 SUMMARY

- The economic way of thinking improves on common sense by looking beneath surface appearances. Faced with a problem, an economist thinks in terms of variables rather than fixed quantities, seeking systematic relationships between these variables in order to predict the outcome as the strength of relationships changes. Theory determines the possibilities: the facts determine the particular outcome.
- Production processes typically involve the combination of many inputs that may be combined in varying proportions. Simple technologies with only two inputs may be depicted by equal product curves or isoquants.
- A level of output may be maintained by substituting one input for another; but as substitution proceeds it gets progressively more difficult. The rate of substitution of one input for another falls.
- Paretian efficiency means that it is not possible to change a situation so that someone is better-off without anyone being worse-off. When combining inputs this involves technological efficiency, the avoidance of waste of resources, and economic

efficiency, the choice of the least cost, technologically efficient, combination.

- Factors of production are usually able to contribute to making a wide range of products. The possibilities of producing two goods from a given supply of inputs may be plotted on a transformation curve. Such curves are typically convex upwards showing the increasing difficulty of substituting one output for another, and hence the increasing cost of expanding one output in terms of its alternatives.
- Economic cost is defined as the most valuable opportunity that has to be given up as a consequence of a particular disposition of resources. This is opportunity cost, a concept that links together all decisions involving resources having alternative uses.
- Economic cost differs from accounting cost in that it is forward-looking and determined by the alternatives available, not by past money payments. When activities are pursued together, any common costs have to be considered as a totality.

7 MEMO

Rocket craft, tank landing-craft decked over to carry a thousand rocket projectors, are not noted for manoeuvrability. Berthing such a vessel can be slow and bumpy. Yet the tale is told of one commanding officer who with a few crisp orders – Port Thirty, Midships, Starboard Twenty, Stop Port, Full Astern Starboard, Midships, Finished With Engines – would bring his craft alongside with the dash of a destroyer captain. Before doing so he would go to his cabin, take a paper from the confidential books safe and study it. The paper read: 'Port is left and starboard is right.'

If an economist kept a reminder of fundamentals on a small piece of paper, it would declare: 'Economic cost is opportunity cost.'[4]

Part II

THE BUSINESS ENVIRONMENT

2

FIRMS, MARKETS AND INDUSTRIES

Business economics involves firms, markets and industries; but not always the firms, markets and industries of everyday conversation. Some distinctions must be made.

1 FIRMS

Lawyers, on-course bookies and accountants have a precise definition of a 'firm'. It is an unincorporated business provided with capital by a single proprietor or by two or more persons in partnership operating under the Partnership Act. Businesses incorporated under the Companies Acts, with capital provided by shareholders, are companies; and businesses set up under special statutes are public corporations.

Economists vary the reference of 'firm' with the problem in hand. Owner-managed businesses, partnerships, joint-stock companies and public corporations may all be regarded as firms for some purposes; but very often parts of such undertakings are taken separately and treated as 'firms', and sometimes co-operative arrangements between independent undertakings are analysed as 'firms'.

Market and administrative integration

Explanation of numbers employed, investment in plant and machinery, stock holdings, prices and output are sought in terms of decisions of managers and workers. The area over which decisions extend is the firm. Firms are thus regarded as areas of unified business planning within which resources are allocated by administrative decision: beyond the boundaries of firms activities are integrated by the market.

It is possible, given sufficient imagination, to think of an economic system without any firms, consisting solely of independent agents responding to price signals so that opportunities for complementary production are taken up, workers distribute themselves between occupations according to their earning abilities, materials go to the highest bidder, plant is hired as needed, and so on. Equally it is possible to conceive of an economic system consisting of one enormous firm, where everything happens in obedience to orders from a central administration. Practical economic systems are found between these two extremes.

Integration by market deals is limited by transaction costs. Buyers and sellers must discover the options available: on the buyer's side, the prices and properties of goods offered, and on the seller's side, the tastes and needs of buyers. Contracts involve repeated expenses of negotiation if short-term, or risky commitments if long-term. Legal enforcement of contracts can be costly. Markets are prodigal with communication costs, spreading information broadly whether people wish to know or not. They are frugal with incentives, proportioning profits and losses to the net excess demand or supply of all participants; but they have nothing more than money to offer. Limitations of market incentives show up where teamwork is involved. Any member of a team may take things easy and, if the rest try hard, enjoy reward without corresponding effort; but what one can do, all cannot.

Administrators are better fitted than markets to measure contributions to team effort, to make sure everyone pulls his weight, and to proportion reward to effort. They have rewards of power and prestige to bestow that may at times be more effective than hard cash. Administrators have some advantages in obtaining information, especially financial information, from within their organisations, and they can make sure that information is addressed to those who need it rather than to the world in general. Costs may, therefore, be reduced by administration, but only up to a point. As areas of administration expand planners become more remote, need more advice before they can reach decisions, must refer matters to and fro, travel to on-site inspections, and confer in more and more committees. As administrative responsibilities grow bigger the possibilities of bigger mistakes also grow bigger, and more and more must be found to pay the people involved.

Boundaries of firms

The broadest boundaries of firms are thus drawn by decision-makers seeking minimum combinations of transaction costs and administrative costs for linking economic activities. These boundaries are temporary. Over time administration becomes routine and managers are released to plan growth, recruit and train additional managers and extend administrative empires. On the other hand, routine may lead into ruts, and organisations may ossify, dwindle and die.

Strategic decisions, such as the disposition of investment funds between different enterprises or the promotion and reward of top managers, encompass the widest administrative domains. A firm in such a context may be a huge multinational, such as Unilever, regarded as a single entity despite its geographical spread, its headquarters divided between London and The Hague, and its multiplicity of processes and products.

When analysing the output and price of a single product, such an all-embracing concept would be inappropriate. Synthetic detergents, soaps, toiletries, cosmetics, margarine, ice-cream and frozen foods are all Unilever products; but it would not be helpful to consider them all together when concerned with the price and output of any one of them. If ice-cream is the subject, it is usually sufficient to take the Walls subsidiary as a separate firm. This procedure gives good results so long as no important joint-costs are involved in manufacture or marketing within multiproduct businesses.

At other times activities for which a number of separate companies are responsible may be analysed as if undertaken by a single firm. The oil and gas industry, for example, is the scene of many joint projects by oil companies seeking to spread the risks of exploration, or to avoid the duplication of refining plant in small markets. Business consortia jointly tender for big construction projects in developing countries. Cartels represent another kind of limited relationship between companies. Companies may jointly agree prices, outputs and productive capacity: such alliances constitute areas of unified decision-making and are conveniently dealt with as 'firms'.

The compass of firms therefore sometimes extends to the largest corporate bodies, sometimes to parts of such bodies taken one at a time, and sometimes to combinations taken all together. We use the expression 'a firm' to represent any collection of business resources – factories, warehouses, machines, materials, employees, patent rights, goodwill, and so on – subject to integrated decisions, in short, an area of unified business planning.

2 MARKETS

'Market' and 'industry' are often synonyms. However, there is advantage in keeping separate a concept embracing suppliers and demanders of closely substitutable goods and services, the market, from one classifying firms by their production capabilities, the industry.

Markets are regular networks of contact between potential buyers and sellers. Some markets, such as those for labour, property and finance, involve firms as buyers and households as sellers. Some involve firms as buyers and also as sellers, for example, markets in raw materials, components and wholesale distribution. Some, most notably those concerned with finished goods, involve households as buyers and firms as sellers.

At times market classifications are broader than those of industries. The market for semi-skilled workers in Sheffield, for example, includes firms operating in steel, heavy engineering, light engineering and houseware industries. Again, the market in sources of primary energy involves firms operating in the coal, oil, natural gas and nuclear fuel industries.

It is more usual for market classifications to be much narrower than those of industries. Most often a market takes in only part of the activities of constituent firms: for example, one would wish to distinguish the market in petrol (gasoline) from that in fuel oil although the same oil companies usually sell in both markets. Single industries are usually concerned with products finding their way into very different markets: for instance, the foundation garments and overcoats of the clothing industry.

Descriptive classification

Markets must be defined so that models may be built for explaining prices and outputs. The simplest scheme is based on ease of entry of sellers, the degree of homogeneity of goods traded, and the number of sellers. A purely competitive market, for example, is characterised by complete freedom of entry, identical products, and large number of suppliers; in heterogeneous oligopoly entry is impeded, products are differentiated by design and presentation, and there are few suppliers. Table 2.1 brings together a number of possible market forms.

It is not difficult to think of markets that fall into these classes. The clearest examples of purely competitive markets are those dealing in financial securities, where there is nothing to choose between one share certificate and another of a particular company and there are lots of potential buyers and sellers. Farm products and primary commodities traded on organised exchanges provide other examples: wheat, barley, oats, rye, rice, eggs, butter, vegetables, tobacco, cotton, wool, jute, natural rubber, and free market supplies of copper, lead, nickel, tin and zinc.

Markets in manufactures are usually oligopolies and occasionally monopolies. To mention a few homogeneous oligopolies, there are the markets in chemicals, plastics, fertilisers, petrol and other oil products. Examples of heterogeneous oligopoly are provided by frozen foods, canned foods, whisky, gin, cigarettes, chocolates, calculators, motor cars, motor vehicle components, TV sets, carpets, carpet machinery, films, soaps and detergents.

Examples of monopolies are not so numerous but they are easily found among public utilities and firms protected by patents. The domestic market in electricity and markets in special prescription drugs are examples. Monopolies also occur where suppliers act together in cartels.

The descriptive classification illustrated in Table 2.1 thus seems a useful one; but it suffers from a degree of ambiguity – how free is free entry? or impeded entry?, how different is considerable product differentiation?, how many are a few sellers? A more

Table 2.1 Descriptive market classification

Market	*Entry condition*	*Product differentiation*	*Number of sellers*
Pure competition	Free	None	Many
Homogeneous oligopoly	Impeded	None	Few
Heterogeneous oligopoly	Impeded	Considerable	Few
Monopoly	Blocked	None	One

.cise classification may be built up in terms of the price elasticity of :mand, cross-elasticity of demand and conjectural price flexibility.

Analytical classification

Ease of entry into a market may be measured by the response of quantity demanded from existing suppliers should price rise above the level providing normal profits. If the elasticity of demand for such a price rise is high it indicates that there are plenty of potential competitors around. The responsiveness of quantity demanded from existing suppliers to a fall in price would depend upon conditions of demand.[1] A monopoly enjoying blockaded entry experiences similar elasticity of demand for price increases and decreases around the monopoly price.

Use of elasticity of demand to indicate entry conditions presumes that membership of a market has already been determined. Membership and degree of product differentiation may be established by price cross-elasticity of demand, that is, the ratio of the percentage change in demand for one commodity to the percentage change in the price of another. The distinguishing feature of items traded in the same market is that buyers regard them as good substitutes for one another, and cross-elasticities are therefore large. When products are homogeneous, cross-elasticities are high and equal between products of all firms. As product differentiation increases, cross-elasticities fall and may not be equal for all pairs of products. The boundaries of markets occur at gaps in chains of substitutability, and are marked by steps down in cross-elasticities between goods inside and outside a market.

Cross-elasticities of demand emphasise the fact that delineation of markets depends upon human behaviour much more than on the technical qualities of goods. For example, the nature of spirits and wine have not changed in post-war years but substitutability between these drinks has increased in Britain to the point where they may be considered part of the same market; on the other hand the cross-elasticity of demand between beer and wine has remained low and beer continues to be a separate market.

Elasticity and cross-elasticity of demand fail to distinguish the main feature of oligopolies. In pure competition and monopoly firms take decisions independently of rivals, in the first case because rivals are too small and numerous to matter, and in the latter because there are no rivals at all. Oligopolies are markets with suppliers who are conscious that success depends not only on their own efforts but also on the way rivals react to those efforts, so that the best thing A can do depends upon what he thinks B will do, and the best thing B can do depends upon what he thinks A thinks he will do, and so on.

Conscious interdependence typically involves small numbers of firms, but the distinguishing feature is not really small numbers but states of mind. The answer to the question how many firms is few enough for oligopoly is the number associated with conscious interdependence. Conscious interdependence may be measured by conjectural price flexibility, which for firm A is the ratio of the expected percentage change in the price of the product of firm B to an actual percentage change in A's price. Conjectural price flexibility is a subjective concept; but this does not mean that it is impractical. If one were to ask the marketing manager for Persil what the reaction of the marketing manager for Ariel would be should the price of Persil be cut, one would be asking a question that could be answered.

Table 2.2 shows a classification of market forms in terms of elasticity and cross-elasticity of demand, and conjectural price flexibility. It will be seen that even the analytical distinctions between markets are distinctions of degree rather than kind. There can be no complete monopolist, for example, because every firm has to compete for the limited purchasing power of consumers and so the cross-elasticity of demand between the monopoly product and others can never reach zero.[2] It is therefore sometimes helpful to think of markets as lying in a triangular space with the ideal types of pure competition, oligopoly and monopoly placed at the three corners, as in Figure 2.1. The width of the sides draws attention to barriers to entry.

Table 2.2 Analytical market classification

Market	*Elasticity of demand*	*Cross-elasticity of demand*	*Conjectural price flexibility*
Pure competition	High	High	Zero
Homogeneous oligopoly	Moderate	High	High
Heterogeneous oligopoly	Moderate	Moderate	High
Monopoly	Low	Near zero	Zero

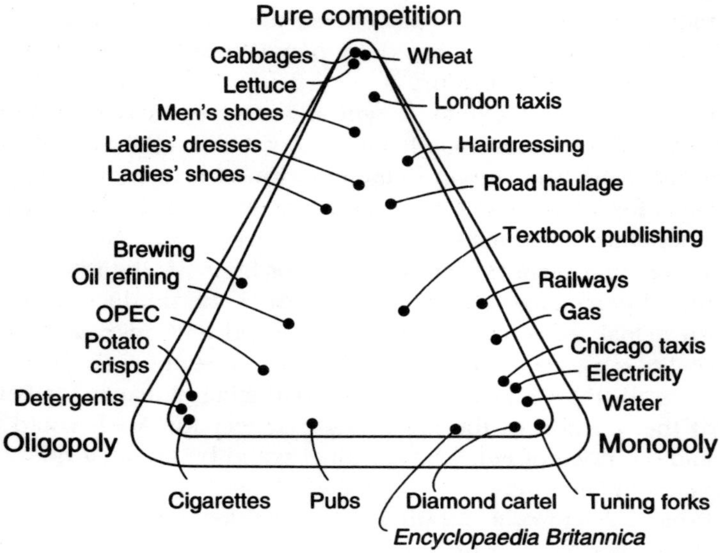

Figure 2.1 A pattern of markets

3 INDUSTRIES

Firms may be classified into industries in many different ways depending on the purpose of the grouping. Eligibility for membership of a trade union, employers' federation or trade association may be established by definition of an industry. Government regulations and subsidies may require legal definitions of industries. Statistics are collected on the basis of the Standard Industrial Classification. Definitions are usually in terms of common technology or know-how. This is the procedure of the Standard Industrial Classification which groups firms according to common raw materials used, such as wool or iron and steel, by common processes, such as brewing, and by products with related methods of manufacture, such as wooden furniture.

Wherever borderlines are drawn it will be found that some firms falling within one industry also undertake activities considered part of another, and even units falling unequivocally within one industry form a heterogeneous collection of undertakings. Moreover, no industrial classification is satisfactory for long. New industries, such as bio-engineering and robotics, are created and firms move from one industry to another as profit beckons.

Industries are important for price theory for two reasons. First, there is the practical consideration that official statistics are usually collected for industries rather than markets. Differences between industries and markets must always be kept in mind if the statistics are not to mislead. The way concentration ratios for industries have been bandied about as measures of competition within markets provides many cautionary examples.

Secondly, industries are a source of new entrants to markets. The extent of competition within individual markets is often underestimated because attention is concentrated on substitutes currently available rather than on potential supplies that could come from firms outside the market but within encompassing industries. For instance, in early post-war years Gillette had more than three-quarters of the British razor-blade market. Its predominant position had been built on the basis of the King Gillette patent, and seemed assured because its production techniques and marketing methods were far in advance of other blade manufacturers. Gillette's position was assaulted by Wilkinson Sword when they introduced a coated stainless steel blade. At the time Wilkinson were manufacturers of garden tools. Gillette and Wilkinson have both had to meet competition from disposable razors introduced by Bic, a ball-pen manufacturer. All three face ever stronger competition from electric razors.

Barriers to entry into a market are sometimes measured by estimating costs that would be incurred in setting up production from scratch. Such estimates fail to take into account the likelihood that entry will come from firms already to be found in surrounding industries.

Joan Robinson summed up the usefulness of industrial classifications:

> The concept of an industry, though amorphous and impossible to demarcate sharply at the edges, is of importance for the theory of competition. It represents the area within which a firm finds it relatively easy to expand as it grows. There are often certain basic processes required for the production of the most diverse commodities (tennis balls, motor tyres and mattresses) and economies in the utilisation

of by-products under one roof. The know-how and trade connections established for one range of products make it easier to add different commodities of the same technical nature to a firm's output than it is to add mutually substitutable commodities of different materials, or made or marketed by radically different methods. Moreover, the members of an industry have common interests and a common language, and feel a kind of patriotism which links them together, even when they are in competition with each other. It is much easier to organise control over one industry serving many markets than over one market served by the products of several industries.[3]

4 SUMMARY

- Firms are areas of unified business planning within which activities are integrated by administration rather than by the unconscious working of market forces.
- Firms enjoy economies in transaction costs that are eventually offset by rising administrative costs.
- Parts of a company may be regarded as 'firms' when costs for particular products can be separated from those of the whole concern.
- Joint activities of a number of companies may be analysed as if they are the responsibility of a single 'firm'.
- Markets are regular networks of contact between potential buyers and sellers.
- Product markets may be classified by entry conditions, product differentiation, and number of sellers, or by elasticity and cross elasticity of demand, and conjectural price flexibility.
- An industry represents an area into which member firms may easily grow once established in one part: an area within which it is possible to replace one product by another with comparative ease: an area where substitutability is easy on the supply side.

3

AIMS OF BUSINESS

1 INTRODUCTION

Most economic models depict a minimising–maximising world. Firms seek to minimise costs and maximise profits, households seek maximum satisfaction. An overriding concern is whether their individual decisions complement one another to satisfy conditions for maximising the total value of output. Is the world really like this? In particular, do firms seek maximum profits?

They may do so because they want to, more money being sought for creature comforts or as an outward and visible sign of achievement, a source of power, and a method of scoring in the business game. They may do so because they have little choice, profit maximisation being necessary for survival in competitive markets, a shield against take-over bids, and a criterion for cohesive decisions in large organisations. But what if a firm enjoys a protected market and salaried managers do not identify their interests with those of shareholders? A number of alternative aims have been suggested for large companies where there is separation of ownership from control.

The next section is devoted to the meaning of profit maximisation, its dependence on future events, long-term nature, uncertainty and consequent subjectivity. Section 3 discusses the way in which objectives are affected by the form of business organisation, owner-management, partnership or public company, and the possibilities of the interests of managers outweighing those of shareholders in joint-stock companies. Section 4 looks at ways in which the need to keep pace with competitors, avoid the threat of take-over, and control large organisations may enforce maximising behaviour irrespective of the wishes of managers or shareholders.

2 THE MEANING OF PROFIT MAXIMISATION

Looking forwards

When we say that a businessman wishes to maximise profit we mean that he wishes to maximise *future* profit. Money profit is determined by the relationship of the future inflowing stream of receipts and future outflowing stream of payments. Maximising profit means arranging matters so that the difference between these two streams is more satisfactory than the difference that could be secured by any alternative arrangement.

Three factors have to be taken into account. First, the amounts of receipts and payments, secondly, the dates when they come in or go out, and thirdly, the certainty with which they can be relied upon. Where a choice of action exists the alternatives may vary in any combination of these factors. Each may secure a different volume of receipts, a different rate of flow, a different degree of certainty; the same applies to payments. This is true of any problem we care to consider: quoting a price, taking an order, introducing a new product, launching an advertising campaign, installing machinery, opening a new plant, choosing to do something or nothing, to do one thing rather than another, to do something on a larger scale rather than a smaller. All such decisions, and any combination of such decisions, call for estimates of the effect on future receipts and payments.

More is implied by profit maximisation than the choice of policy yielding the biggest difference between receipts and costs here and now. Usually it is the long-term profit that matters. Even when the effects on prospective receipts and costs of all alternatives are taken into account it is still not possible to say which is the profit-maximising decision. We still need to know the attitude of the decision-maker towards risk-taking.

Long-term and short-term profit

A particular course of action may result in increased receipts or decreased expenditure in the near future but only at the cost of decreased receipts or increased expenditure in the more distant future. Estimating profit involves weighing up all the consequences of an action, short-term and long-term. Misunderstanding of this point may cause business people to deny that their aim is profit maximisation. It is not profitable, save in very unusual situations, to snatch an excess of receipts over payments of £5,000 next month if the consequence is loss of an opportunity for an excess of receipts over payments of £50,000 next year.

Account must be taken of the 'goodwill' of a business. Businessmen and businesswomen usually take pride in their products and want the public to benefit from them. They may enjoy a craftsman's satisfaction in quality and insist on high technical standards. They may value a reputation for honest dealing with suppliers and customers, for good relations with employees, for a good wage record, for generous treatment of workers on retirement, and so on. They see their companies progressing towards distant time horizons.

The problems of estimating long-term effects and of allowing for the fact that receipts and payments in the future are not the same as receipts and payments now, that is, of discounting, may and usually do make it difficult to reduce profit estimation to tidy arithmetic; but the elements of the sum may be taken into account even if they are not reduced to a simple answer. Some of the alternative aims considered later cease to conflict with profit maximisation when maximum profit allows for long-term influences.

Attitudes to risk-bearing

Comparing alternatives is not only a matter of judgement and arithmetic. It is also a matter of personal preferences. Experts may agree or disagree about the likelihood of certain results following certain actions. They can argue about the facts, the influences, the probabilities. They can narrow the issue to the point where it is possible to say what differences in assumptions are responsible for differences in estimates, and they can debate the validity of the assumptions. When these arguments have been fully thrashed out a decision has to be taken as to which set of possibilities and uncertainties is to be preferred, and one factor in this choice is the decision-taker's attitude to risk-bearing. Suppose that two courses are open and that on the best estimates available the first course will yield between £300,000 and £400,000, whereas the second will yield between £100,000 and £600,000. The choice depends upon how much certainty of income is to be sacrificed for how much possible additional income. Choices often present different degrees of risk and individuals vary in their taste for risk.

It is possible to formalise some of these subjective attitudes and compare decisions in each formal model. For example, a pessimist who believes the worst will always happen sees profit maximisation as making the best of things when the worst happens. His objective is to maximise the minimum gain attainable from alternative decisions: he has a maximin objective. A Panglossian, believing all is for the best in the best of all possible worlds, will press ahead in the hope of maximising the maximum gain: he has a maximax objective. A third possibility is to take account of the regret that will be felt if it turns out that a bigger profit could have been attained by a different decision. Someone in this frame of mind sees profit maximising as minimising the maximum regret: the objective is minimum regret.

The subjective elements in profit maximisation loom even larger when attention is directed to aims within different forms of organisation, and the possibilities of conflicting aims of the people involved.

3 FORMS OF ORGANISATION

So far we have talked of business people without making any attempt to define who we mean. A business consists of men and women who come together to provide collectively goods or services. Some provide the organisation with work in exchange for wages and salaries; some provide materials, machinery and equipment in return for outright payment; some provide buildings for rent; and some provide finance, enabling the gap to be bridged between payments and receipts, bearing the risk that the gap will not be bridged, and enjoying the profit (or some of the profit) when it is. This last group, the 'capitalists', are traditionally seen as the group who mainly determine the aims of a business. It is they who by deciding whether to make finance available decide whether there shall be a business at all.

Owner-managers

Decision-making is at its simplest where there is only one capitalist. When there is only one proprietor it is necessary to keep proprietor and business distinct. Often the undertaking is organised as a private limited company, but even in the case of an unincorporated business it is necessary to separate business life from private life.

Owner-managers are generally controlled and disciplined in their business decisions. Indeed it is commonly argued that standards of conduct inside and outside business are different, usually to the disadvantage of the former. Be that as it may, the dividing lines between people and their businesses are real. There are two reasons for this. First, nearly everybody feels that no matter how unbusinesslike they may be in their private affairs they must be businesslike in business, taking the not-unhealthy view that income had better be earned before it is spent. Secondly, if the business is of any size, it has to be run in co-operation of others and this co-operation is only possible after organisational aims have been set.

However, businessmen are still men, or with increasing frequency women. As Walter Bagehot commented: 'if a businessman is always busy it's a sign of something wrong'. Some pursue profit with unflagging energy, sacrificing all leisure short of that needed to stay healthy and often being prepared to go even further. But they are not typical.

Typical behaviour was first put in diagrammatic form by T. Scitovsky, and his argument is worth noting because it takes the form followed by many later analyses of aims conflicting with maximum profits.[1] There is seen to be a trade-off between profits and some other desirable end, in the present case between profits and leisure.

In Figure 3.1, profits are measured vertically and leisure horizontally. In any period of time, say a month, a businessman or woman has a total amount of time, OM, available for all purposes. Time devoted to work is measured leftwards from M (more work, less leisure). It is assumed that output increases with time devoted to it, and that larger outputs at first yield increasing profits but that beyond some point profits fall because of increasing production and marketing costs and lower prices. Profits therefore reach a peak when MA is devoted to business, leaving OA for the rest of life. If no account is taken of lost leisure, the proprietor would have horizontal indifference curves and would choose to work MA hours; but if leisure is regarded as a good, indifference curves between profits and leisure have a more usual shape and MC hours are devoted to work, aiming at profits of CD instead of the maximum AB.

Allowing for golf courses makes less difference to the analysis than might appear at first sight. No matter what the golf handicap,

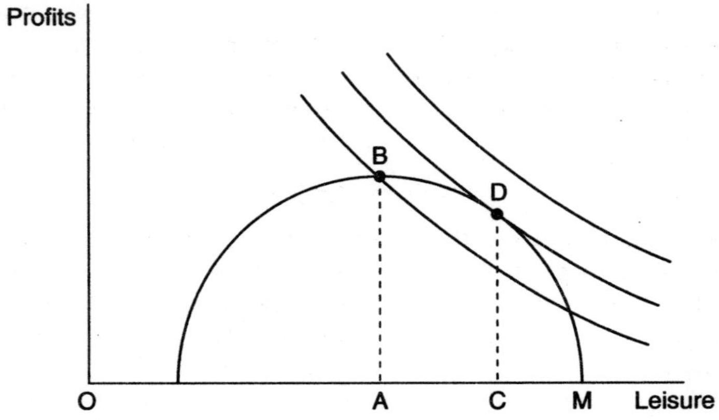

Figure 3.1 Trading profits for leisure

the response to changes in costs, sales prospects, technology and so on is likely to be the same as that of the most devoted work slave.

Partnerships

Partners must also decide how much time to devote to profit-making; but they can no longer decide on their own. The aims of partners must be reconciled. Many partnerships have come to grief because this was not, or perhaps could not, be done.

Suppose a firm of publishers has three partners: one wishes to build up the reputation of the firm as a publisher of educational works and is prepared to sacrifice short-run profits to do so, the second wants a reputation for beautifully produced books and the third wants money quickly. It is possible, though unlikely, that the business can be run on lines to satisfy completely all three partners. More probably there will have to be some give and take, and objectives and strategy will have to be clearly formulated to express an agreed compromise. If this is not done there will be woolliness, muddle and frustration.

As the number of capitalists increases, the possibility of conscious compromise becomes less. In a very large partnership the objectives are usually determined by those with the largest shareholdings, the greatest seniority or the strongest personalities. There are many examples of firms that cannot be reorganised until the senior partner retires or dies. In such cases junior partners are little more than salaried employees with a bonus related to profits. They accept the dictates of their seniors until they in turn move up the scale and are able to point the firm in the direction they favour.

Public companies

In limited companies with few shareholders the position is much the same as in the case of partnerships. When there is a majority shareholding one would expect the ownership interest to prevail in setting objectives. In large companies a minority of shares is often sufficient to give control.

A rough order of magnitude is that large companies have as many shareholders as they have employees, and so they usually have many small shareholders. This augments the power of the larger capitalists remaining. Much less than 51 per cent of the equity is needed for control when shares are widely distributed, demonstrating the power of a determined minority. Consider three shareholders, each owning one-third of the ordinary shares, who are called upon from time to time to choose between two courses of action, A and B: the first shareholder always favours course A whilst the other two vote at random. In this situation the first shareholder will get his way 75 per cent of the time although he has only 33.3 per cent of the votes. Voting would go:

1st shareholder	*2nd shareholder*	*3rd shareholder*
A	A	A
A	A	B
A	B	A
A	B	B

The power of minority shareholdings is augmented by small shareholders usually giving their proxy votes to directors, and so whoever has the power to appoint and unseat directors can determine the objectives of a public company. It turns out, partly because large companies are often successors to owner-controlled companies, that 5 per cent of the ordinary shares in one hand suffices for the ownership interest to prevail in setting profit as the main objective to be pursued.

Proprietary interests may prevail with even greater dispersion of shares. S. Nyman and A. Silberston cite the case of Debenhams, where there were no shareholdings as large as 5 per cent.[2] In 1970, after a long period of poor performance, a group of institutional investors, none of whom owned a significant percentage of shares, intervened to secure the appointment of a new chairman. Within four years a new chief executive had been appointed and seven directors, out of a board of ten, had been replaced. Institutions may be equally influential when they show disapproval by selling shares rather than intervening directly. When they vote with their feet they do so in giant-sized boots.

Nyman and Silberston investigated control of the top 250 companies in *The Times* 1,000 for 1975. Defining potential ownership-control as at least 5 per cent of the voting shares in the hands of the board of directors, a single institution or cohesive group, or the presence of a member of the founding family as chairman or managing director when no shareholdings amounted to 5 per cent, they found that 55.5 per cent were owner-controlled. The position varied a good deal between industries with food, drink, metal manufacture, electrical engineering, construction, retailing, merchanting and miscellaneous services being predominantly owner-controlled, and tobacco, oil, chemicals, metal goods (not elsewhere specified) and building materials being predominantly non-owner-controlled. The position is changing rapidly as financial institutions, such as pension funds, insurance companies, unit trusts and investment trusts, become the most important owners of shares in the bigger companies.

It is sometimes suggested that institutional investors, especially pension funds, are mainly interested in regular dividend payments and so support short-term against long-term objectives. This is unproven, and is not very likely. First, if the capital market is efficient, prices of capital assets should reflect long-term prospects as well as short-term dividend payments and institutions should be indifferent between capital appreciation and dividends of like amount. Secondly, institutions control very diversified portfolios of shares, and so face smaller risks with their portfolios than those facing individual joint-stock companies they partly own. They should therefore favour greater risks associated with long-term projects than may be the case within individual companies. The main worry with institutional investors is that they may be better informed of the accounting record of companies than of the fundamentals that determine their long-term prospects.

What of the 44.5 per cent of the largest companies with no

preponderant shareholding interest? The Debenhams case suggests caution in jumping to conclusions, but in many of these companies power must rest with the directors. Although they are formally appointed by the shareholders and can be dismissed by them, directors are usually co-opted to the board by existing members and the appointment ratified by acquiescent proxy-voters. This could give directors wide areas of discretion. In so far as non-monetary aims influence the affairs of great companies, it is the directors, their characters, their prejudices and their motives that are the source of such aims.

Directors and top officials of large concerns often reject in their statements and actions the criterion of profit maximisation. Commonly they see their responsibility as something broader and based on obligations, beyond legal and contractual ones, to workpeople, customers, the community in general, and to the organisation itself. Since these obligations are at some points obscure and at others in conflict, what happens in particular circumstances depends upon the relative strength with which each obligation is felt by the person involved and how far he rates the obligation above profits.

Growth

A number of attempts have been made to produce generalisations about management behaviour in these circumstances. R. Marris has suggested that top management in large companies pay attention to two indicators, the market price of shares as an indicator of shareholder satisfaction, and the long-run growth rate of total assets as an indicator of management satisfaction. Management may sacrifice some profits for growth, but not too much because finance for growth depends upon retained profits and subscriptions to new shares which are only forthcoming if profits, dividends and share prices are maintained.[3] Managers are seen as trading-off share price against growth, as in Figure 3.2 which has the ratio of market-value of shares to book value of assets on the vertical axis and percentage growth of assets on the horizontal axis; the indifference curves are those envisaged for the board of directors.

The Marris model captures an element of management motivation. There never was a manager who did not check the market price of his company's shares in the paper each morning,

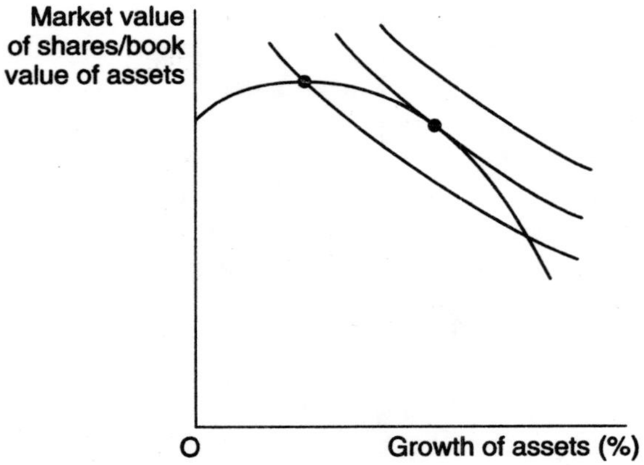

Figure 3.2 The Marris trade-off

and it makes sense for attention to be paid to the ratio of market value of shares to book value of assets because the lower it is the greater the threat of take-over. The difficulty is to separate Marris motivation from profit maximisation. Long-term profits depend upon growth, and it may be advantageous to forgo immediate profit and invest more than simple financial criteria might suggest because growth is good for morale and boosting productivity. A Marris firm may invest more than a profit-maximising firm but in other respects is likely to react to changed conditions in similar ways to those of a profit-maximising firm.

Sales maximisation

W.J. Baumol has suggested that modern managements seek to maximise sales or growth of sales, subject to profits being at an acceptable level, rather than maximise profits. His model is illustrated in Figure 3.3, where maximum profit is attained at output OA, but output OC is preferred. Profits are once again sacrificed, this time for sales, but again only within limits, among other reasons, because retained profits are needed to promote future sales.[4]

Sales maximisation captures another element that may be present among managerial objectives. Managers can usually say what last month's sales were and seldom what last month's profits

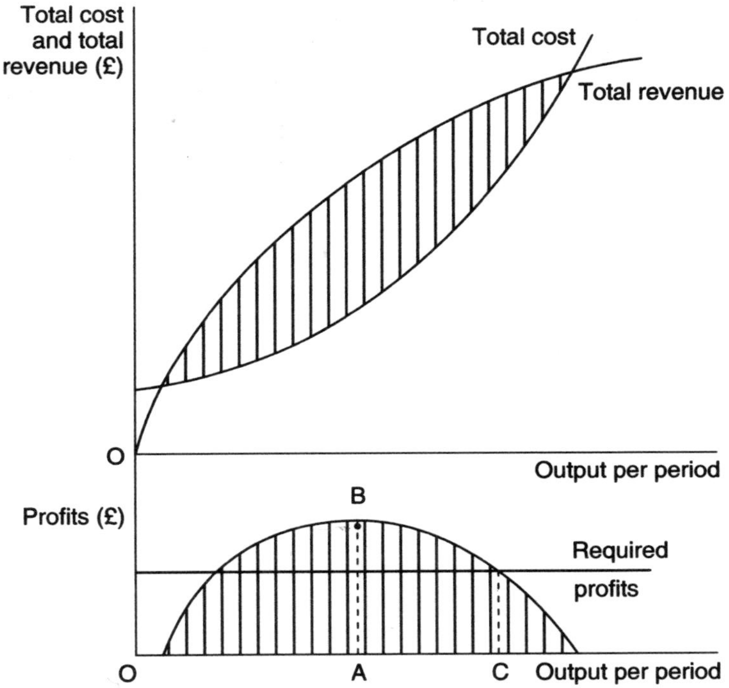

Figure 3.3 Baumol's sales-maximisation model

were. When there are small numbers of competitors they are usually well aware of their own and others' market shares. Moreover, aiming at market share may well be the best short-term objective for securing long-term profit. It has the merit of looking outwards, focusing attention on the customer and his needs.

It is difficult to be sure of the difference between sales maximisation and maximising long-run profits. Baumol provides a possible explanation of advertising budgets that seem high for the increased sales attained. A sales-maximising firm would react in the same direction as a profit-maximising firm to an increase in demand or increase in costs. However, a tax on undistributed profits would lead to a contraction in output in order to meet the profit constraint although it would not affect the output chosen by a profit-maximising firm.

Managerial perquisites

O.E. Williamson has developed a model based directly on the special interests of management: given that earnings and dividends are sufficient to satisfy shareholders, the management are envisaged as seeking subordinates to confer status and support future operations, amenities to make business life more pleasant, and retained profits which may be used in the business at their discretion. Directors and top managers in this case seek maximum profits in production activities, but less than maximum profits overall because of the employment of additional staff and provision of fringe benefits for managers.[5]

Satisficing

Marris, Baumol and Williamson all provide qualifications to profit-maximising behaviour. H.A. Simon has argued that all maximising theories are unrealistic: management, he asserts, lack the information, information-processing capability and inclination to maximise. Managers do not seek the best solution, they are content with a satisfactory one.[6] This certainly has a realistic ring, and could represent a radical departure in theorising. However, the difference between satisficing and maximising may not be as great as appears at first sight. Psychologists argue that aspiration levels are reduced if there are successive failures in attempts to reach them, and aspiration levels are raised if they are easily reached. Satisficing may thus be a step-by-step approach to maximisation.

Satisficing theories lay emphasis on the cost of securing information needed for the best solution; but such costs enter into calculations of profit-maximising firms. Profit maximisation does not prescribe spending more on improving a decision than the improvement would be worth.

There is no shortage of alternatives to profit maximisation and qualifications of profit maximisation. Nevertheless we are going to build explanations and analysis on the assumption that firms attempt to maximise profits. This is done partly because it provides a first approximation that may be adjusted to take account of other considerations, but mainly because there are forces at work impelling firms to attempt to maximise profits whether managements wish to or not. Managements face external and internal constraints on the policies they may pursue.

4 PRESSURES FOR PROFIT MAXIMISATION

When competition is keen firms will not succeed in earning the market rate of return on their capital if they fail to aim for the maximum profit attainable, and when competition is weaker managements cannot allow themselves much leeway with the assets they control lest they become targets for take-over bids. In addition to pressures from outside, firms are pushed towards profit maximisation by the need to reconcile the decisions of specialist and subordinate managers and to provide unambiguous directives for delegated authority within the management hierarchy.

Competition

Most businesses face competition from rivals. When managers have to bend all their efforts to ensuring that their products are of the right quality and price to earn enough revenue to meet outgoings, other private ends that they might like to pursue, but which conflict with profit maximisation, can only be sought at the expense of the margin efficient performance allows. They cannot be pursued out of comfortably earned profit, part of which might be sacrificed with no great qualms.

A desire to adopt a labour policy which offers shorter hours or higher pay than the general market, a desire to improve quality or raise the standard of design to a level which in the customers' view is not worth the extra cost, a desire for increased advertising to enhance a company's image, a desire for the latest plant irrespective of its return, a desire to run the business in a part of the country that cannot offer advantages obtainable elsewhere, a desire for a quiet life and avoidance of anxiety, these and many other wishes, good and bad, can be indulged only to the extent that owners are prepared to pay. When competition is strong, in the long run efficiency will yield only a normal return on capital, and in such cases the price of pursuing private aims may be high.

The further we get from competitive conditions, and the easier it is to avoid losses and make profits, the more can business people indulge in aims that are inconsistent with profit maximisation. This is a complicating factor in large undertakings with considerable monopoly power. However, in the private sector, no matter how secure managers may be from competition in product markets, they may still be obliged to aim at maximum returns lest control be wrested away in a take-over bid.

Take-overs

The market value of shares in a company depends upon the current and prospective internal rate of return on assets, the policy with regard to retaining profits and anticipated growth of assets, and the market rate of discount on future earnings. An outsider, usually another company, might apply a lower rate of discount than the market, possibly because of a different evaluation of risks, and so would value the company at more than the market. There would be gain from taking over the company provided that the deal could be financed. Similarly, if an outsider considers that a larger internal return could be obtained on the assets, possibly by more single-minded pursuit of maximum profit, then once again his valuation will exceed that of the market and there will be the possibility of an attractive take-over.

There is nothing a management can do to protect itself from the first kind of take-over, but the second can be avoided by successful efforts to maximise profits. The assignment of officers within large companies to financial analysis of public companies shows that they are looking over other companies' shoulders, and when doing so cannot but be aware that other companies are likely to be looking over their own. Merger activity tends to come in waves, and it may well be that take-overs will become less fashionable, but the possibility of losing control to more profit-conscious outsiders remains a force making for widespread pursuit of maximum profit.

Delegation

In large companies there are also forces working within the business, stemming from the need to ensure coherent direction and control, which support profit maximisation. When a business becomes large enough for some decision-making to be delegated the definition of aims must be faced. In a small business where a manager can see all that is going on, the problem of ensuring that decisions are in line with aims is fairly easy. The larger the business, and the larger the measure of delegated responsibility, the more important it is to ensure that aims are clearly understood.

Responsibility for decisions can be adequately discharged only if those who have to make decisions know the criteria to adopt.

In many instances conflicts between sub-optima aimed at by middle managers and the grand optimum aimed at by top managers do not arise. For example, the works manager in making the best use of floor space, the purchasing agent in determining when and how much raw material to buy, the sales manager in determining discount policy or quoting prices in competitive markets, and the plant manager in choosing machine tools and settling replacement questions may rarely be faced with decisions where other aims conflict with the profit test. However, conflicts can arise.

The natural inclination of specialist managers is to place emphasis on technique for its own sake: engineers like long runs of production, sales managers wide variety of output, personnel managers contentment on the shop-floor, finance managers rapid cash-flow, and so on. Logically, if the consequences of decisions are to be compared with one another there must be some common unit into which they can all be converted. The only available unit is the monetary one: comparison may be made of the consequences for flows of money costs and money receipts. As General Motors pointed out in an oft-misunderstood moment, they are in the business of making money not of making automobiles.

The larger and more complex the business the more carefully its operations must be planned in order to ensure that it functions coherently. Hence the main decisions are likely to be made at intervals through agreed budgets, usually after considerable discussion of alternatives by top management. Those in command are likely to prefer their subordinates to work for maximum profit, reserving for themselves decisions of a major character where profit-making and other aims conflict. In this way they ensure compatibility of decisions within their organisation, improve ability to meet competition, and ward off possible take-over bids.

5 SUMMARY

- Profit maximisation is forward-looking: it depends upon future flows of receipts and payments that may vary in amount, timing and certainty. Maximum profit is therefore a subjective concept which can vary from maximising the minimum gain, through minimising regret to maximising the maximum imaginable profit.

- There are a wide range of aims that may conflict with profit maximisation. The analysis of such conflicts usually takes the form of a trade-off, for example, the trade-off between profits and leisure.
- The extent of the divorce between ownership and control in large joint-stock companies is often exaggerated, and is being reduced by the increasing reach of finance capital.
- A small percentage of ordinary shares is usually sufficient to ensure control on behalf of the ownership interest because of the power of resolute minorities and also because of the willingness of proxy voters to support the controlling interest.
- Special managerial theories of business aims, such as Marris's theory that managers trade off growth against the market value of shares, Baumol's that managers seek maximum sales subject to a profits constraint, and Williamson's that managers trade off profits against perks, can only be pursued in firms insulated from outside pressures.
- Satisficing may amount to much the same as maximising when account is taken of the costs of decision-making and of the adjustment of aspiration levels to attainment.
- Despite all qualifications, the profits test remains the most important single controlling factor in business decisions. It may be imposed by competition or the threat of take-over, and it may be a logical necessity with delegated responsibility.

Part III

PRODUCT MARKETS

4

THREE MEANINGS OF COMPETITION

Economists' attitude towards competition is much as to motherhood: even the orphans are in favour. This is partly because competition has so many connotations. Three meanings of competition – as an activity, a social process, and a market structure – deserve special consideration.

1 COMPETITIVE ACTIVITY

Samuel Johnson defines competition in his *Dictionary*: 'Competition. n.s. (*con* and *petitio*, Latin) 1. The act of endeavouring to gain what another endeavours to gain at the same time, rivalry, contest.' And Ambrose Bierce in his *Devil's Dictionary* defines a competitor as ' a scoundrel who desires that which *we* desire'. Competing as striving to do better than rivals, to run the race, win the game, to succeed, is what governments usually have in mind when they adopt policies to promote competition. They seldom have ambitions to create economies satisfying the conditions of pure competition but see competitive activity as a means for improving productivity, promoting change and economic progress. This may involve price competition but, equally important, it involves search for new products and processes, innovation, imitation and provision of wider choices to consumers and workers.

Incentives to search are important because production possibilities and consumers' preferences are not known in advance. Competitive activity involves seeking out opportunities rather than passively adapting to them, and this often means introducing new products and methods of production, or imitating successful innovators so that progress is diffused throughout the economy. This leads to widening choices for producers and consumers.

The importance of choice is something we become aware of when it is not available: if there is only one supplier you are at his mercy; if there are two they are each at yours. Choice gives power which may be measured by all the things that could be done should one wish.

Competitive activity is not confined to particular market structures. It can be found in purely competitive markets, although competitors in such markets are limited to reducing costs in order to get ahead of other suppliers. It can equally be found in markets with small numbers of suppliers where competitors are reluctant to precipitate price wars, but instead seek to get ahead of one another by product innovation, process improvements, advertising and sales promotion. Evidence of active competition may be provided by price-lists; but equally it may be provided by such things as the extent of product improvements, changing market positions of products and market shares of firms. The increasing durability of car engines, car tyres and lubricants, all innovations that reduce the size of the total market whilst offering better value for money, bear witness to competitive activity by product improvement within markets dominated by very large firms.

Competition in pharmaceuticals

Figure 4.1 shows the changing ranking of three categories of medicines, and displays active competition in markets where patents have sometimes seemed to provide excessive protection against competitors. Medicines acting on the lower respiratory system are clearly no substitutes for those treating rheumatism or heart conditions. These three medical areas provide three distinct markets. It may be seen that there is considerable movement in the market positions of the main suppliers in each market over quite a short period of time.

It might be argued that competitive activity is better analysed within the wider industry. Although medicines for the three conditions are not substitutes for one another, it is possible for firms producing for one market to discover and develop preparations for other markets. Figure 4.2 shows the ranking of the top twenty pharmaceutical companies over a longer period. It is clear that as the first company in 1962 fell to fifteenth in 1970, the second in 1962 fell out of the top twenty, the fifteenth in 1962 rose to second in 1970, and so on, there was active competition between these companies.[1]

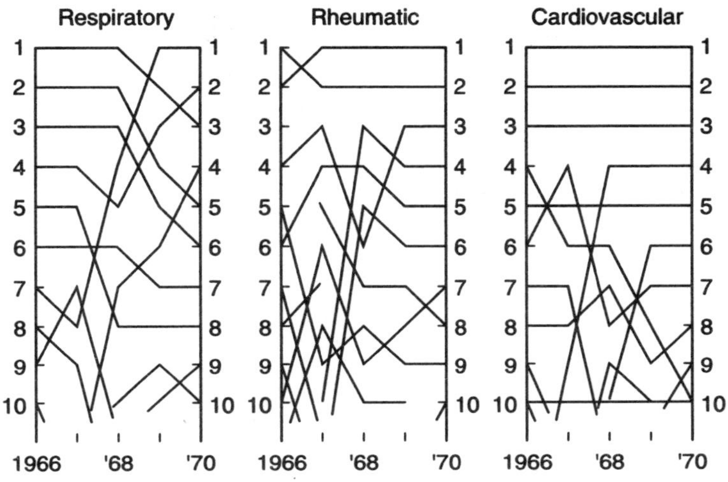

Figure 4.1 Ranking of top ten companies in three medical areas
Source: NEDO, *Focus on pharmaceuticals*, London, HMSO, 1972

This interpretation is difficult to challenge; but it does not wholly dispel uneasiness about the cost of drugs or the profits from patents such as those for Librium and Valium. Part of the trouble is that many things were changing in morbidity and medicine whilst the market positions of suppliers fluctuated. Conviction would come if *other things were equal*.

Competition and numbers

The main method of partial equilibrium analysis is to take a market where all participants have fully adjusted to prevailing conditions and to deduce changes that would be brought about by a change in one of those conditions, *other things being equal*. It is seldom possible to conduct experiments to check whether deductions are correct, and equally rare to find situations that differ in only one respect so that comparisons may be made. Other things are not usually equal; but occasionally life imitates science. Shortly after the Second World War, Lord Bauer and B.S. Yamey found not just two but tens of geographically separate markets that were similar in most respects but which differed in one significant way.[2]

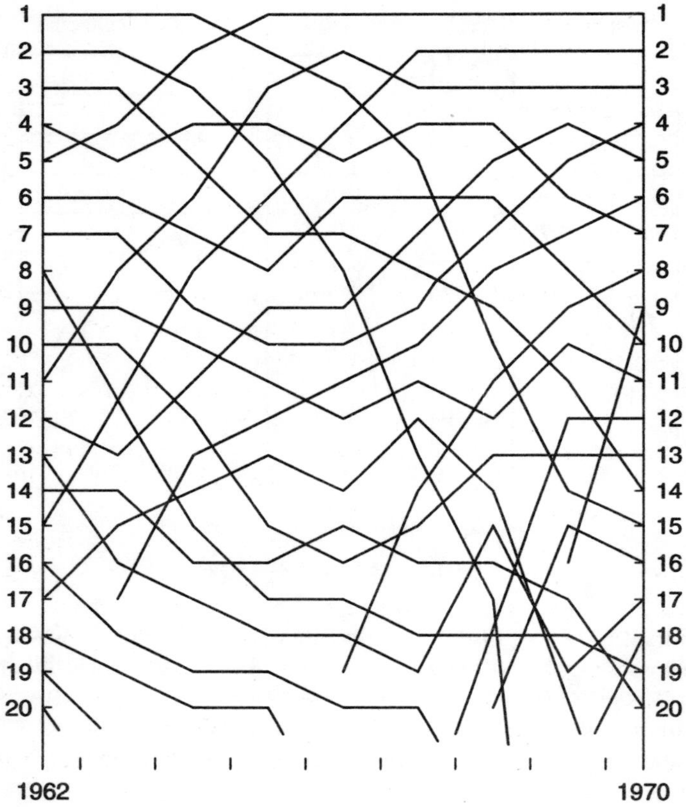

Figure 4.2 Ranking of top twenty companies in UK prescription market

Source: As for Figure 4.1

In the closing years of the British Empire, colonial administrators began to intervene actively in economic affairs to protect the interests, as they saw them, of the native population. In Nigeria they set up the Groundnuts Marketing Board to guarantee minimum prices to growers. The Board did not buy groundnuts directly but instead licensed trading companies to act on its behalf. Minimum buying prices were prescribed for a large number of buying stations in the northern area, accounting for more than 90 per cent of the crop, and in the rivers area around the upper Niger and Benue. In 1949–50, along the railway line in the north, the minimum price was fixed at £21.20 per ton, along one river the minimum was £20 and along the other £19. Away from railway line or river at road stations lower minima were laid down, the difference in price being intended to provide for extra transport costs. Licensed buying agents received the railway or river price plus a block allowance of £4.50–4.90 to cover costs of bags, interest, insurance, overheads, commissions and salaries.

It might be thought that licensed buying agents would pay growers no more than the statutory minima. On the other hand, if transport allowance exceeded actual transport costs or if block allowance exceeded operating costs, they would make extra profit on every extra ton bought and might bid up the price to obtain more supplies. What happened? In the rivers area the minimum price was paid at every buying station. In the north the minimum price was exceeded at almost every buying station. At thirty-two buying stations away from the railway line, overpayments ranged from £0.05 to £4.25 per ton, and averaged £1.28. How could this be? One answer is that in the rivers area 80 per cent of purchases were made at stations where only one buying agent operated, and there were only two agents covering the entire area. In the north there were twenty-one buying agents.

The influence of numbers of competitors on prices paid may be seen in more detail at nine buying stations along the railway. At these stations all buying agents were required to pay the same minimum price, and received the same block allowance. The number of buying agents at these stations and average overpayments are shown in Table 4.1.

Table 4.1 Payments above statutory minima

Station	*Number of licensed buying agents*	*Average overpayment (p/ton)*
A	1	0
B	2	0
C	2	0
D	2	50
E	3	55
F	4	30
G	6	80
H	7	30
I	10	100

At six of the nine stations there were overpayments, and the largest overpayment was made at the station with the largest number of buying agents. However, the relationship between numbers and strength of competition is not an exact one. It may be suspected that other things were not quite equal, and such proves to be the case. At D there were only two buyers yet 50p overpayment per ton, and at E there were only three buyers and 55p overpayment, but one firm was a newcomer in each market. At H there was only a modest overpayment and six of the seven agents belonged to a buying syndicate. There was also a buying syndicate at I to which all the agents belonged, but seven represented European firms and three represented Levantine firms.

This research, therefore, shows that the intensity of price competition increases with the number of competitors, but that entry of new firms is also important, and competition is increased when firms come from different backgrounds. It is evident that in the absence of competition, as in the rivers area, government intervention may be needed to protect against monopoly; but active competition, as in the north, may be more effective than administrative protection. Notice that the firms making payments above the legal minima were large, sophisticated, mostly expatriate companies, and the people receiving overpayments were poor, illiterate peasant farmers. Active competition thus provides a social mechanism for protecting the weak. Some have seen it performing a wider social role.

2 COMPETITION AS A SOCIAL PROCESS

When firms strive to do better than one another, some win and some lose. Those attaining lower costs, offering better value for money, more attractive goods and services, survive and laggards go to the wall. Those best able to satisfy customers are discovered by a Darwinian social process. Hopefully, the fittest survive.

This idea that competition is a selective process adopting business ventures that contribute most to satisfying wants and rejecting firms that fail the market test, is apt to be attractive to successful businessmen. John D. Rockefeller, for example, maintained that 'the growth of a large business is merely a survival of the fittest . . . The American Beauty rose can be produced in the splendor and fragrance which brings cheer to its beholder only by sacrificing the early buds which grew around it. This is not an evil tendency in business. It is merely the working out of a law of nature and a law of God.'[3] The Almighty is sometimes seen as rewarding the bold, enterprising and energetic, and offering little consolation to the timid, dull and lazy. It is difficult for those not possessing the first set of virtues to deny their importance; but, just as Darwinian evolution may be the consequence of accidental mutations fitting into ecological niches, the competitive selection process may at times reward luck rather than virtue.

When a large proportion of a market is supplied by a small number of very big firms, it is often presumed that the big firms must have been managed much better than the rest; but this need not always be the case. It is instructive to look at the market structure that chance alone might produce. Figure 4.3 shows the distribution of output between seventy firms when chance has been at work for thirty-five years. The eight largest firms produce 61 per cent of total output, and the 80–20 rule holds (80 per cent of the output is produced by 20 per cent of the firms). Yet this distribution has been brought about by chance.

In year 0 we begin with 128 firms all of the same size with output, x. Every five years they face equal chances of output doubling or halving, and if output falls below 0.5x they drop out of the market.

Although the outcome for any one firm is purely a matter of chance the process need not be an arbitrary one. The firms that double in size may do so for what, after the event, seem good reasons: they may have happened upon processes, products or marketing techniques that best suit the market. The competitive selection process may therefore be one of rewarding the fittest or of discovering the fittest. In practice the system selects for effort and luck in varying proportions.[4]

3 COMPETITIVE MARKET STRUCTURES

Competitive activities and competitive social processes are only loosely connected to competitive market structures. It is possible to think of competitive activity as taking place within market structures, and of the whole as constituting a social process; but this is an incomplete picture as some competitive activity is directed to changing market structures.

'Pure competition' and 'perfect competition' are market structures with special significance in economic analysis. Remember that

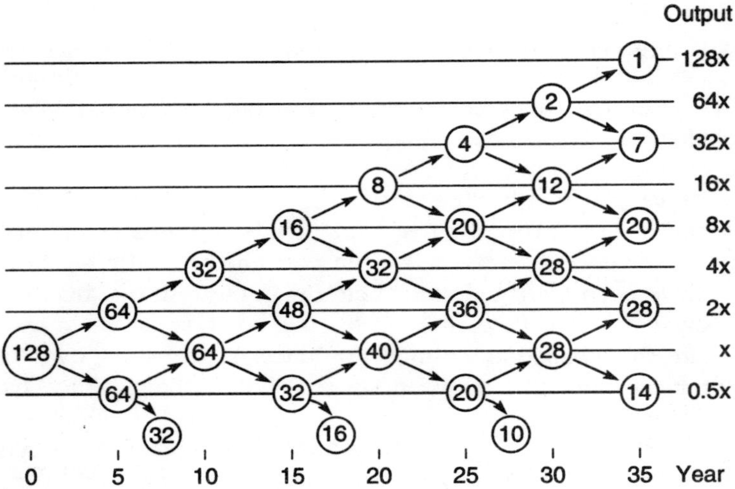

Figure 4.3 A model of chance, growth and survival

these are theoretical categories: there is nothing specially virginal about pure competition or morally worthy about perfect competition.[5] Pure competition refers to markets with (1) freedom of entry, (2) large numbers of suppliers and demanders, and (3) homogeneous products. Perfect competition refers to markets having these three characteristics plus (4) complete mobility of factors of production and products, and (5) complete knowledge possessed by all participants of prices and conditions affecting demand and supply in all parts of the market.

Pure competition may seem a bit remote from everyday experience, but this is a parochial view. The mass of humanity are peasants producing homogeneous goods along with lots of others for lots of customers. Even when governments intervene in agricultural markets, the model of pure competition is needed to analyse the effects of such intervention. Some markets for manufactures, such as clothing and leather goods, would fall into the purely competitive category if account were only taken of domestic suppliers and demanders; but it must be remembered that most manufactures enjoy foreign markets and are subject to competition from imports so that the numbers involved in trade for most goods are larger than appears at first sight. Furthermore, account must be taken of potential competitors able to enter a market should it prove exceptionally profitable.

The importance of potential competition has been emphasised repeatedly by P.W.S. Andrews and Elizabeth Brunner. Much analysis assumes that competition only threatens from new firms, new legal entities installing new capacity:[6]

> This would appear to go back to static pure-competition analysis, with the marginal firm waiting in the wings, as it were, smaller, more ignorant, less efficient than firms already established in the industry. But Andrews has pointed out the importance of cross-entry competition, i.e. firms already established in other product markets who can move into this market. These may be firms in quite a different industry which are seeking diversification. It may be a firm integrating backwards to control its supply of materials, or integrating forwards to control its immediate market. It may be a firm already in the same industry, but moving into a market which it was not in before.[7]

W. Baumol, J. Panzer and R. Willig have given great emphasis to one aspect of potential competition with their concept of perfectly contestable markets. A perfectly contestable market is one which firms can enter and, if they wish, leave without losing money invested, that is, a market that does not require specialised capital. Capital requirements may be large as with aircraft, but it may be possible to use the equipment to supply a variety of markets. Contestable markets perform in similar fashion to purely competitive ones, for example, abnormal profits are only temporary.[8]

An important feature of competitive markets is that changes in demand or costs do not lead to permanently enhanced or depleted profits: the response to abnormally high profits is expansion of output by existing firms and entry of new suppliers until profits return to a normal level, and the response to losses is contraction of output and exit of firms. This is illustrated in the next chapter by some experiences of the London taxicab trade.

Perfect competition is a more restricted theoretical model than pure competition. The assumption of perfect knowledge of all market opportunities by all participants seems to carry abstract thought to extremes; but this assumption may not be as demanding as appears at first sight. Competitive markets provide a means of mobilising the knowledge spread throughout the community.

When some people are trading in ignorance of the true situation they provide opportunities for the more knowledgeable to make profits; but the latter can only profit by removing the influence of ignorance so that market prices reach levels that would hold if everyone were well informed from the outset.

It is usually difficult to assess the knowledge possessed by participants in a market as they do not broadcast what they do and do not know. However, there is one market, that providing gambles on horse races, where everyone is obliged to disclose his or her knowledge or ignorance when laying a bet before a race begins, and we can test whether market-odds accurately reflect horses' chances. This thought leads on to stock exchanges and the efficiency of financial markets in the next chapter. Some of the problems of organising knowledge by market processes are examined in Chapter 8.

4 SUMMARY

- Competition may refer to an activity: contending in the market, vying with other firms for custom, searching for and exploiting market opportunities. Offers of better value for money, product and process innovations, and changing market shares of products or producers, all bear witness to such activity.
- Competition may, secondly, refer to a process of social selection in which effort receives reward or rejection according to its profitability. Luck plays a part in survival in the business as in the biological world.
- A third possibility is that competition may refer to a state of affairs, a market structure such as pure competition, defined by freedom of entry, numbers of participants and homogeneity of products. Freedom of entry means that account must be taken of potential competitors as well as those currently supplying a market.

5

PURE COMPETITION, PERFECT COMPETITION AND EFFICIENT MARKETS

1 INTRODUCTION

The essential feature of markets satisfying the conditions of pure or perfect competition is that sellers and buyers are *price-takers* who are forced to accept market prices. Their collective behaviour determines the level of price, but their individual decisions have no identifiable impact on that level: as they see it, prices are fixed by impersonal market forces, all a matter of demand and supply. The individual competitors see themselves as having to contend with the market, not with each other. If they were given to thinking in geometrical terms, suppliers would see their individual demand curves as horizontal lines and demanders would see their individual supply curves as horizontal lines.

This follows from product homogeneity and from the large numbers of sellers and buyers involved. When there is a homogeneous product there can only be one price at any time and place: no one can find a buyer at more than the market price and no one can find a seller at less than the market price.[1] When there are large numbers of sellers and buyers, all small relative to the size of the market, no individual can have a perceptible influence on market conditions. Suppose there are 10,000 suppliers of equal size and one increases his output by 100 per cent, total output would increase by 0.01 per cent.

Pure and perfect competition share a third assumption of freedom of entry and exit for suppliers. This means that profits cannot be above or below the level of a normal return on capital in the long run. The response to losses or abnormal profits is contraction or expansion in the number of suppliers. Freedom of entry also implies that there are potential suppliers to take into account in addition to those currently serving a market.

Perfect competition refers to market structures with two further features: complete mobility of factors of production and products, and possession of complete knowledge of all market opportunities by all members of the market. The addition of these two assumptions depends upon the purpose of analysis. Mathematical economists generally prefer the precise results obtainable with the additional assumptions; but their presence or absence makes less difference than might seem at first sight. The existence of immobilities may be allowed for by introducing transport costs. When transport costs are low, movement of the products of factor services may act as a substitute for movement of factors. Competition organises knowledge spread throughout a market, providing price signals of shortage or surplus and profit incentives to overcome the one or dispose of the other.

This chapter spells out the implications of competitive market structures. Section 2 examines the nature of short-run adjustments of competitive firms aiming to maximise 'quasi-rents' so as to make the largest possible contribution to overheads and profits. The third section discusses long-run equilibrium and the part played by economic rent. Section 4 emphasises the point that competitive markets adjust to losses by exit of firms and to abnormal profits by the entry of firms, so that profits tend to a normal level in the long run. Two episodes in the history of the London taxicab trade provide illustrations. Section 5 is devoted to perfect competition in betting shops and the Stock Exchange. The exchange of contingent claims between punters and bookmakers, and of financial securities between investors and stockbrokers, involve trivial transport costs. In both areas there are elaborate arrangements to provide information about the goods traded and the state of trade at any one time. An efficient market is defined as one where prices fully reflect all knowledge relevant to buyers and sellers as soon as it becomes available. It is therefore of interest to enquire whether perfect competition leads to market efficiency.

2 SHORT-RUN ADJUSTMENTS AND QUASI-RENTS

In the short run, firms are free to vary the intensity with which they use productive capacity, but that capacity is assumed to be constant. There are two reasons for giving such situations separate analysis. First, it provides an explanation of short-run supply and so contributes to an understanding of price fluctuations. Secondly, it explains why firms may continue production whilst proclaiming that they are producing at a loss. This may not be masochism, but sound common sense.

In the short run, firms must cover their variable costs or they would be better off not producing at all. Beyond variable costs they hope for the largest possible contribution to overheads and profit. This contribution, the excess of receipts over variable costs, is 'quasi-rent'. The technical term stems from the special meaning of economic rent as a payment which is larger than that required by a supplier if he is to continue to supply, that is, a payment greater than opportunity cost. Economic rents accrue to factors of production that are in fixed supply and that have only one use or one use in which they are exceptionally productive. In the short run fixed factors are in given supply and are committed to a particular line of production. Hence any payment they receive is economic rent, but rent of a short duration or quasi-rent. A lasting economic rent has a market value equal to the capitalised value of future rents; quasi-rents do not last long enough to be capitalised.

As a matter of mathematics, not of how business people may or may not think, the most profitable decision for a firm is to produce the output at which marginal cost equals marginal receipts: if additional output adds more to receipts than to costs, the added output improves the situation; if it adds more to costs than to receipts, it worsens the situation; and when it adds the same amount to receipts and costs, the best output has been attained. In pure competition individual firms face a given market price at which they can sell whatever they wish, each additional unit of output adding its given price to receipts. Marginal receipts per unit of output therefore equal price, and the best a single firm can do is to produce the output at which marginal cost equals price. Possible short-run equilibria at different prices are shown in Figure 5.1.

It may be seen that at price p_1, the output at which marginal cost equals price is q_1, which is also the output at which average cost equals price. At q_1 total receipts equal total costs Op_1Aq_1, and these receipts are therefore just sufficient to cover variable costs plus fixed costs (including normal profit). Quasi-rent, not shown in the diagram, just equals fixed cost, the difference between total cost and total variable cost. At a higher price p_2, the firm would produce output q_2 at which its average total cost per unit is less than its receipts per unit (the price p_2), and in consequence would receive abnormal profit. The firm would earn a quasi-rent of Dp_2BC which

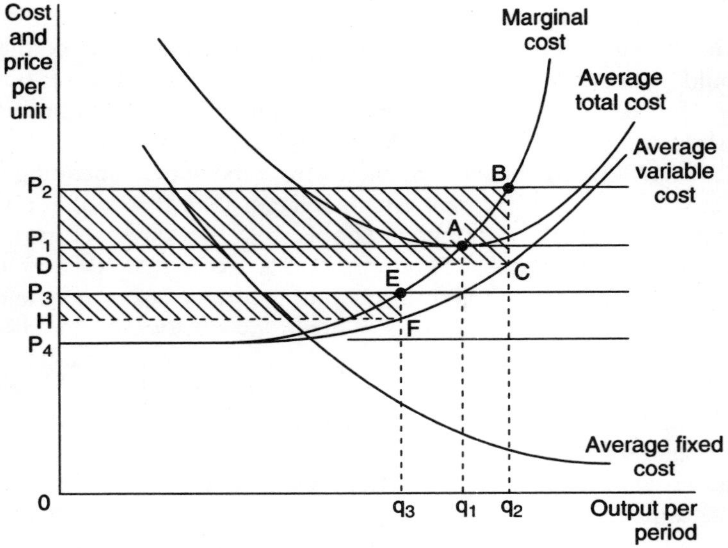

Figure 5.1 Short-run equilibria and quasi-rents

more than covers fixed cost. At price p_3, the best the firm could do would be to produce q_3, at which output it would receive quasi-rent of Hp_3EF that is insufficient to cover fixed cost. It would not, of course, choose such output for ever. Eventually plant and equipment would need replacing, the short run would be over, and at price p_3 replacement would not be worth while. At prices below p_4, the firm would produce nothing in the short run.

Prices corresponding to p_1, p_2, p_3 and less than p_4 have been seen in the oil tanker market since 1970. Freight rates reached a peak during the Arab–Israel War, declined with the re-opening of the Suez Canal, fell further with contracting oil trade associated with high OPEC prices and world depression, and eventually were insufficient to cover operating costs of a large proportion of the world fleet. At the end of 1984, 46 million dead-weight tons of oil tankers, 19 per cent of the commercial fleet, were laid up awaiting better times.

3 LONG-RUN EQUILIBRIA: SUPPLY AND ECONOMIC RENT

Assuming away differences

Quasi-rents arise in the short run. In long-run analysis it is tempting to assume conditions that exclude economic rent as well as quasi-rent. If all firms are able to use the same techniques of production and can buy inputs of the same efficiency on the same terms, economic rents do not appear. In such conditions all firms in the long run have identical costs and, so long as factor prices do not change, supply to the market is perfectly elastic at a price equal to minimum average cost of each firm. When demand increases additional firms enter the market, and when demand decreases some firms leave. If all firms produce at the same minimum average cost it is not difficult to demonstrate that all firms are of optimum size and total costs of supply are minimised.

Recognising differences

However, managers, workers and inanimate inputs are not of uniform efficiency, and some of them are specially suited to particular kinds of production. In these circumstances economic rent may occur in the long run. In the long run all inputs are variable and receipts must cover opportunity costs of all inputs, including normal profit on capital employed; but receipts may be greater and in long-run equilibria provide economic rent. Economic rent arises when firms are unable to employ factors of uniform efficiency because of inelasticities in the supply of factors, and it can only be recognised when the market viewpoint of all suppliers considered collectively is distinguished from the separate viewpoints of individual firms.

Economic rent may accrue to any kind of factor of production in fixed supply with a single use or, less restrictively, to any factor in inelastic supply with a specialised use. It is not confined to land, but we take land for illustration. Suppose that there are four kinds of land available for growing wheat. If not used for growing wheat, all four kinds would yield annually £200 per hectare in the best alternative use, that is, £200 after covering all costs except land. The opportunity cost of land to the wheat market is therefore £200 per hectare. At the going price of wheat, the land least suited to wheat would yield £180 per year in wheat. At this price such land is thus extra-marginal to the wheat market: it would yield more in the alternative use. The second kind yields £200, the third £220, and the fourth £240. The second kind is marginal to the wheat market, just worth using for wheat, whereas the third and fourth kinds are infra-marginal. At the going price of wheat, farmers would have to pay market rents of £240 per hectare for the best wheat land, £220 for the second-best, and £200 for the remaining two kinds, or corresponding capital sums should they choose to buy rather than rent land. Anyone offering less than these market rents would have his offer refused because it would be worth while for competitors to pay the full net yield of the land.

From the point of view of individual farmers, the market rent would appear to be an opportunity cost, representing the value of the land to some alternative user. However, from the collective market viewpoint, it can be seen that the market rents of the two better kinds of wheat-land are made up of two elements, an opportunity cost of £200 plus economic rent of £40 for the best land and £20 for the second-best. The land would still be devoted to growing wheat whether economic rents accrued or not, so long as the yield covered the opportunity cost to the market. At a higher price of wheat, the fourth grade of land would shift to wheat growing, the third would become infra-marginal and yield economic rent, and economic rents for the better grades of land would increase.

Long-run supply

The reason for making these distinctions between market rent, economic rent and opportunity cost to the market may be seen in the derivation of long-run supply. In Figure 5.2a we let the market consist of only four firms for convenience of illustration. In the long run there are no fixed costs, so there are only average and marginal costs to consider. These are shown with all inputs valued at opportunity cost to the market, excluding economic rent. So long as opportunity costs are covered supplies are forthcoming. At a price equal to its minimum average cost each firm would supply the quantity at which average cost reaches the minimum, and at higher prices would supply quantities that bring long-run marginal cost into equality with price. It may be seen that at price p_1 the fourth firm is extra-marginal because minimum average cost exceeds

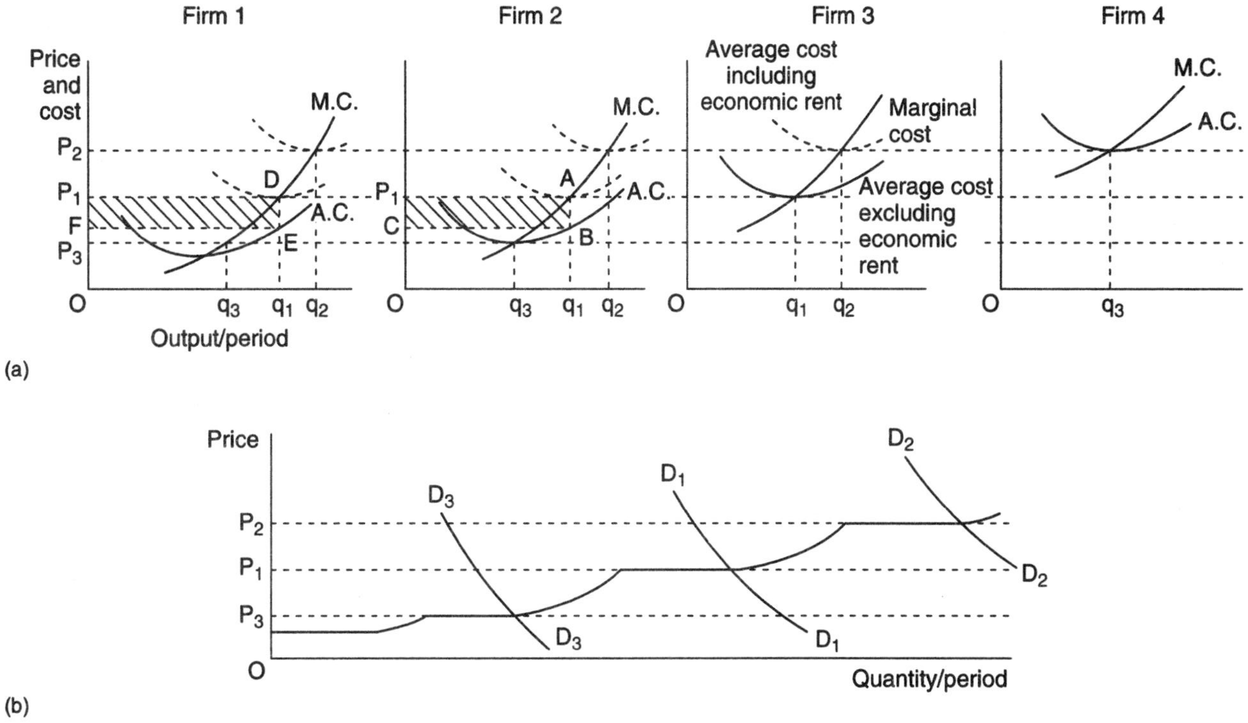

Figure 5.2 (a) Average costs excluding and including economic rent (b) Long-run supply derived from (a)

the price. The third firm is marginal with opportunity cost just covered, whilst the second and first firms produce output at which p_1 is greater than average cost. These two firms receive economic rents of p_1ABC and p_1DEF respectively.

Dashed curves show average costs when costs are calculated including economic rent. When economic rents are included, all firms producing do so at minimum average cost; but when economic rents are excluded only marginal firms operate at minimum average cost.

If the price rises, marginal firms become infra-marginal and all infra-marginal firms increase output to the point where marginal cost equals price. Additional suppliers, extra-marginal at the lower price, begin production. At price p_2, the fourth firm enters and becomes the marginal firm supplying Oq_2: the third, formerly marginal firm, increases output from Oq_1 to Oq_2, and the other firms also increase output. Economic rents rise for infra-marginal suppliers. If the price falls, marginal firms become extra-marginal and leave the market, whilst the remaining firms reduce output. At price p_3, the price is insufficient to cover opportunity costs of firm 3 and it would cease production: firms 2 and 1 would reduce output and only firm 1 would be left with some economic rent.

The market supply is the sum of quantities produced by all firms at alternative prices. The supply curve plots these quantities as in Figure 5.2b. It can be seen that market supply depends upon costs excluding economic rent, the receipt and size of economic rents being determined by the level of price. The elasticity of the supply curve depends upon the steepness of the rise in marginal cost above minimum average cost in supplying firms, and the difference in minimum average cost in existing and potential suppliers. If marginal costs increase slowly and the cost ladder of minimum average costs is shallow, the long-run supply curve will be elastic. In Figure 5.2b, three demand curves have been added showing the determination by demand and supply of prices p_1, p_2 and p_3.

Features of long-run equilibria

Five features of long-run equilibria deserve notice:

1. The allocation of output between firms is efficient.
2. Economic rent determines the merit order in which firms enter or leave the market.

3. Firms that are marginal to a market are not necessarily less efficient than infra-marginal firms.
4. A firm may face problems should market demand fall even though it is an infra-marginal firm.
5. The main beneficiaries or sufferers from government interventions in markets are apt to be the recipients of economic rent.

Let us look at each of these features in turn.

First, in competitive equilibrium it is not possible to reduce the cost of market supplies by reallocating output between firms. Each firm produces an output at which marginal cost equals price. If output were taken away from one firm and given to another, the marginal cost in the first firm would fall below price and that of the second rise above price: the saving of cost in the first firm would be less than the addition to costs in the second. This efficiency characteristic of competitive markets follows from all firms being price-takers.

Secondly, although economic rent may appear to be passive, being price determined and not price determining, it has an active role to play in competitive markets. The efficient use of resources depends upon their being employed by those able to put them to their most valued use. Firms show that they are the most appropriate stewards of resources by paying the full market price, including economic rent, of the inputs they use.

Thirdly, despite the fact that marginal firms earn no economic rent, this need not mean that they are less efficient than infra-marginal firms. It may simply be that the opportunity costs of the inputs they employ are greater than the opportunity costs of the inputs into infra-marginal firms. In the example above, opportunity cost to the market was the same for all kinds of wheat-growing land; but this need not be the case. The absence of economic rent may result from high suitability of inputs for other products as well as low suitability for the product under consideration.

Fourthly, being infra-marginal suggests that a firm is out of trouble, inboard rather than overboard; but life may not be so simple. If a firm borrows to finance assets valued partly because they yield economic rent, if product prices fall it may be unable to meet its debt obligations. It may be forced into liquidation, and its assets may be bought by another firm at a valuation corresponding to the lower product price. Bankruptcy may therefore force a firm out of business but leave its assets for continued use by a new owner.

Fifthly, it is never clear whether governments intend to benefit the people who actually gain from their policies or the people whom they proclaim they are assisting. For example, since 1939 successive British governments, whether in or out of the European Union, have shown great concern for the prosperity of agriculture. Did they really intend that land prices should increase forty-fold between 1939 and 1985, or did they have the incomes of working farmers in mind? In the event, farmers' incomes have done no more than keep pace with average incomes, but land prices have rocketed. This is the kind of outcome to be expected when policies increase demand for particular products. Inputs that are limited in supply and specialised to these products rise in value to allow for increasing economic rent. Policies benefit those who have the wisdom or good fortune to own such inputs at the beginning. People buying such inputs later are obliged to pay the full market price, including enhanced economic rent, and may suffer should policy be reversed even though they have enjoyed none of the earlier benefits.

Further insight into the operation of pure competition may be gained by examining purely competitive markets. One such market is that for the services of London's cabbies.

4 PURE COMPETITION AND THE LONDON CAB TRADE

Market structure

The assumptions of pure competition fit the London cab trade very closely. First, there is freedom of entry. The Metropolitan Police are required to issue licences to ply for hire to any cabs that satisfy their conditions for safety and manoeuvrability. They are also required to issue driving licences to any applicant who passes their driving test and knowledge of London test. There are no restrictions on the number of cabs or drivers. Secondly, there are large numbers of suppliers and demanders. In post-war years there have never been fewer than 5,000 cabs operating. Thirdly, the product is homogeneous: there is nothing to choose between one cab and another. Passengers take the first cab on the rank, the first cruising by, or the nearest radio-cab.

This purely competitive market is not allowed to operate in complete freedom. In addition to police regulation of the quality of cabs and cabbies, there is control of fares by the Home Secretary who prescribes tariffs registered on taximeters. Involvement of the Home Office with the trade has meant that when problems have arisen committees of enquiry have been appointed. Two committees, the Runciman Committee reporting in 1953, and the Stamp Committee, reporting in 1970, are of special interest.[2]

Short-run disequilibrium

In the early post-war years the cab trade ran into considerable difficulties. In 1946, there were 5,620 cabs on the streets and numbers increased steadily to the end of 1950 when there were almost 7,000 cabs; but in January 1951 decline set in and by the end of 1952 numbers had fallen below the level at the end of the war. The number of cabs fell by 20 per cent in two years. The cab trade was clearly not in equilibrium, and the Runciman Committee was called upon to investigate and make recommendations.

The Committee reported just before the 1953 budget, and its main proposal was implemented in the budget. Having the benefit of hindsight, we may see whether the committee were right in their diagnosis and prescription.

Costs and equilibrium

At the end of 1952, 41 per cent of cabs were owned by owner-drivers and 59 per cent by proprietors, mainly small operators, owning more than one cab. Proprietors' cabs were mostly driven by journeyman drivers who worked for 37.5 per cent of metered fares plus tips and any extras for additional passengers and luggage. The proprietors received 62.5 per cent of registered fares and met the costs of providing and running their cabs.

A proprietor would continue to operate his cabs so long as his share of receipts covered costs that varied with mileage, such as petrol, tyres, accessories and repairs, together with other inescapable costs, such as insurance, road tax and meter rent. These costs increased repeatedly, especially with the heavy taxation of petrol. Cabs would not be replaced when worn out if proprietors' receipts failed to cover total costs including interest and depreciation. Many replacement decisions had to be made because the cab fleet contained a good number of ancient cabs inherited from pre-war days. Any motorist knows that interest and depreciation make up a large part of his annual motoring costs. In the case of the cab trade they amounted to about 20 per cent of total costs, and they were not being covered by receipts.

The Runciman Committee argued that the slump in the trade would be self-righting as receipts per cab would increase with increases in engaged miles enjoyed by a reduced number of cabs. However, they thought that the corrective process would be speeded up if the price of new cabs could be reduced. Accordingly they recommended that the 33.3 per cent purchase tax should be removed from new taxicabs.[3] This proposal was adopted within one week, which is some kind of record. The number of cabs stabilised and then began to grow as costs were reduced with the introduction of diesel engines and demand grew with rising incomes.

Minicabs, taxicabs, profits and growth

By the mid-1960s the number of cabs had increased to more than 7,000, when the trade began to protest loudly about unfair competition by minicabs. Minicabs got their name from some highly publicised imports of small Renault cars but despite their name are usually large private cars. They are not able to ply for public hire, but gain clients by telephone. As they are engaged in private hire, cars and drivers are free from the special licensing arrangements and price controls of taxicabs. Hence the charges of unfairness which the Stamp Committee was appointed to investigate.

Proprietors and cabbies have an abiding sense of grievance because of their special relationship with the Metropolitan Police; but there is no doubt about the reality of their new sense of grievance with minicabs. These provided very visible competition when they discharged passengers at a number of favourite locations, such as London airport and the main railway terminals; but when the Stamp Committee looked into competition they found that, apart from some prominent places, there was little overlap between the trade of minicabs and taxis. Minicabs operated mainly in the outer ring of Greater London, more than five miles from the centre, whereas taxicabs found most of their fares within five miles of the centre. When the size of the cab trade is examined it turns out that the number of cabs was increasing throughout the period of complaint about competition from minicabs. It may well be that the cab trade would have been even more prosperous without the competition of minicabs; but it can scarcely be argued that it was ailing when owner-drivers and proprietors saw an advantage in adding 1,400 cabs to the existing fleet.

Restrictive licensing and capitalisation of economic rent

In good times and bad, taxi firms have two unvarying proposals for improving their lot: limit the number of cabs and raise the fares. These proposals show a grasp of economic realities. Provided market demand has an elasticity of unity or less, total receipts do not suffer with higher fares, and if fewer cabs enjoy the receipts, these happy few must be better off. Sir Roy Allen provided evidence to the Runciman Committee pointing to an elasticity of less than unity, so fewer cabs and higher fares are a road to riches.[4] However, these proposals would only benefit people owning cabs when restrictions were introduced. If licences were transferable they would acquire a market value equal to the capital value of the prospective economic rents to which they would give title. This may be seen in a number of provincial cities where the number of taxi licences is limited and cars with a licence sell at a premium over comparable second-hand cars without licences. It is demonstrated in most spectacular fashion in New York, where the number of license medallions has not been increased since 1936: in 1990, tax medallions had a market value of $125,000.

Knowledge of market opportunities is easily acquired in the London cab trade. Everyone knows the price of a journey because it is prescribed by the Home Secretary, cabbies learn the cruising patterns that attract the greatest number of fares, and passengers learn the most likely spots to catch a disengaged cab. In other competitive markets transactions are directed through organised exchanges so that price information is immediately available to all participants, and other information is provided through specialised channels. Newspapers provide sports pages and city pages, and in this way help to ensure that markets provided by betting shops and stock exchanges satisfy the assumptions of perfect, not simply pure, competition.

5 EFFICIENT MARKETS: THE TURF AND THE STOCK EXCHANGE

When knowledge is readily available to buyers and sellers, prices should reflect such information fully and immediately. The assertion that prices in organised markets do indeed reflect all available information is known by financial theorists as the Efficient Market Hypothesis. It is given this tentative title because it is difficult to measure the information marketers possess and relate this information directly to prices. There is, however, one market where beliefs are brought out into the open by its very nature. It is not so formally organised as the Stock Exchange, but a pin is as useful in the one market as the other. The market concerned is that accommodating bets on horse races. As will be seen, the potency of pins is a test for the efficiency of markets.

Horse racing

Gambling is a worrying subject, not only for punters and priests but also for economists. The expected value of a bet is always negative because of the need to provide bookmakers with a living and to pay betting tax. Yet there is no shortage of gamblers, only a shortage of rich ones.

Everyone, except bookmakers, knows that there are no poor bookies, and professional bookmakers do not gamble. They make a book, that is they attract bets by offering odds and adjust these odds according to the weight of betting, so that their book always contains enough field money to pay out on winners and leave a margin for expenses and profits. Bookmakers quote the odds but the odds themselves are determined by the bets people make. The bets are laid in the light of knowledge of past records of horses, jockeys and trainers, form books, racing papers, tipsters, touts, the condition of the course, how the horses look on the day, and in some cases inside information, possibly corrupt, about the running of a race. If punters believe that the chance of a horse winning is better than that shown in the odds they will bet on that horse and its odds will shorten. In the opposite case, fewer bets will be made and the odds will lengthen. Does this process lead to odds that represent actual chances? If so, the betting market must reflect all there is to be known: it must be efficient.

Notice that odds of 6 to 4 against a horse winning is a way of saying that it is believed that the horse has a 40 per cent chance of winning. If it were to run a hundred races in similar conditions it would be likely to win forty. If all probabilities are taken into account they must add up to 100 per cent certainty. In a two-horse race, if one horse has a 40 per cent chance of winning, the other must have a 60 per cent chance.

In the Gold Cup at Ascot in 1984 there were nine runners, and their starting prices are given in the first column of Table 5.1. In the second column these odds are converted into 'probabilities'. It will be seen that the 'probabilities' add up to 109.5 instead of 100. This is normal as the excess provides bookmakers with their margin. In the third column, the 'probabilities' are adjusted for the bookmakers' margin by recalculating them out of 109.5. These are the probabilities of each horse winning that emerged in the market. In the process of betting, Gildoran opened at 8 to 1 and closed at 10 to 1; Ore opened at 7 to 2 and closed at 4 to 1; Neustrien opened at 12 to 1 and touched 16 to 1 before closing at 14 to 1; and so on. Most gamblers were wrong about this race: the favourite, Prince of Peace, came fourth. However, individual races do not prove anything about the ability of the betting market to produce odds that represent actual chances.

If the market is efficient in generating prices, horses assigned a

Table 5.1 The Ascot Gold Cup, 1984

		Starting price	*'Probability of winning'*	*Adjusted probability*
1st	Gildoran	10 to 1	9.1	8.3
2nd	Ore	4 to 1	20.0	18.3
3rd	Condell	12 to 1	7.7	7.0
	Prince of Peace	5 to 2	28.6	26.2
	Karadar	4 to 1	20.0	18.3
	Balitou	12 to 1	7.7	7.0
	Neustrien	14 to 1	6.7	6.1
	Pretty Picture	50 to 1	2.0	1.8
	Fubyman Du Tenu	12 to 1	7.7	7.0
			109.5	100.0

Source: Sporting Life, *Flat results in full, 1984*, Mirror Group Newspapers, London, 1984, p. 217

25 per cent probability of winning will win 25 per cent of the time, horses assigned a 10 per cent probability of winning will win 10 per cent of the time, and so on. J. Dowie analysed all 2,777 races during the 1973 flat racing season, involving 29,307 runners.[5] He standardised starting prices to exclude the bookmakers' margins, converted starting prices into probabilities, and compared probabilities with actual percentages of horses winning. For example, 611 horses were assigned a 20 per cent probability of winning by the market and 21 per cent of them actually won. Dowie's results are illustrated in Figure 5.3, where probabilities assigned by the odds are plotted along the vertical axis and actual winning percentages along the horizontal axis. If the betting market were completely efficient all the points would lie along a 45-degree line through the origin. It can be seen that the betting market is pretty efficient.

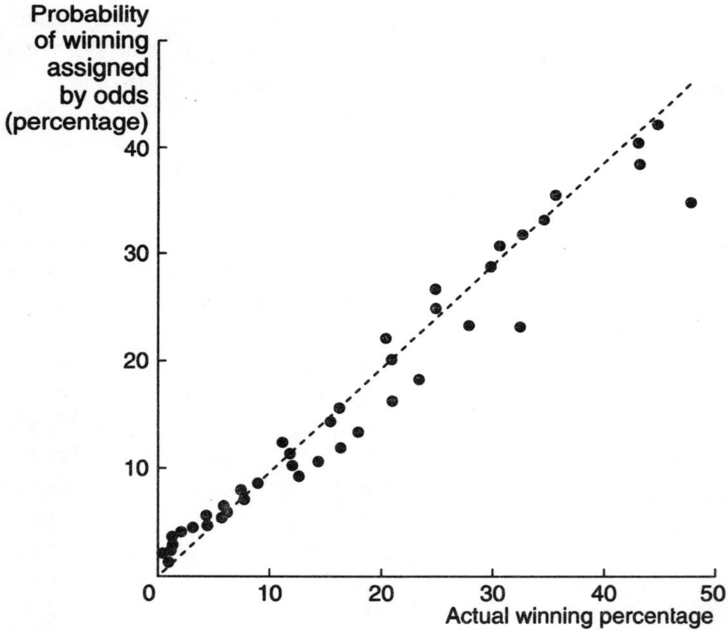

Figure 5.3 Comparing odds and winners

Source: J.A. Dowie (see note 5)

As the market assigns probabilities of winning accurately, a punter with a pin will do no worse over time than a gambler who devotes all his waking hours to studying form. The latter can do no more than estimate accurately the chances of individual horses winning, and the normal working of the betting market produces such probabilities anyway. There is a paradox here. The market will only be efficient in reflecting all information bearing on chances so long as sufficient gamblers give serious thought to their operations. Everyone cannot rely on a pin. The same applies to the Stock Exchange.

The Stock Exchange

Buyers and sellers on the Stock Exchange seek to trade for securities at prices that accurately reflect all available information bearing on future returns and the risks involved: no buyer wishes to pay more and no seller wishes to receive less. There is considerable evidence that the impersonal process of buying order competing with buying order and selling offer competing with selling offer within a perfectly competitive market structure generates such prices, that the Stock Exchange is an efficient information-processing system.

Any computer buff knows that one test of efficiency is the speed with which new information is processed. The Exchange cannot match microchips, but it is remarkably quick. The radio news of commercial events such as exchange rate changes, bank lending rate adjustments, publication of company results, and so on, is usually accompanied by the announcement of consequent changes in share prices. Speed has been more formally tested by analyses of the speed of market reaction to such diverse items of news as mergers, stockbrokers' recommendations, rights issues, and balance of payments figures; they have shown that information is quickly reflected without bias in security prices.

The fact that all information has been absorbed by the end of a trading day may be seen by comparing each day's closing prices with those of the next day. If all information has been taken into account, prices will not change until new information is received. This may be good or bad for shares but there is no way of knowing in advance, and as a result share prices change up and down from day to day in a random fashion. All possible combinations of changes up and up, up and down, down and down, and down and up, appear with almost equal frequency. This random walk of share prices has become well recognised since Sir Maurice Kendall drew attention to it some forty years ago.[6]

Notice that random short-period price changes occur because traders on the Stock Exchange devote so much thought to their purchases and sales. The random walk means that it is a waste of time drawing charts to discover patterns in price changes, or devising systems for short-run share speculation. A pin will serve better.

Share prices would follow a random walk provided traders took account of all current information whether they interpreted that information correctly or not. No doubt prices overadjust and underadjust as information is digested; but there is no evidence of bias in market responses, and the prices turn out to be best estimates of the value of shares. This may be seen in the record of expertly managed portfolios of shares. The experts cannot regularly pick winners, that is, undervalued shares, because sellers are anxious to receive full value, and cannot regularly dispose of losers, that is, overvalued shares, because buyers do not wish to pay too much.

In 1974, the Consumers' Association reported in *Money Which?* on their tests of 274 unit trusts.[7] They found that the comparative performance of a trust in one year was no guide to its performance in the next, or any other, year; no management company did consistently better than any other; there was nothing to choose between trusts managed by stockbrokers, merchant banks, insurance companies, High Street banks and specialist firms; capital trusts and income trusts performed similarly over time; and there was no relationship between the size of fund and its average performance. The Consumers' Association concluded:

> We found that the average general unit trust performed somewhat better than the *Financial Times* Actuaries All-Share Index over the five years to mid-February 1974 (after allowing for tax, income, and share buying and selling costs). Looking at each of the five years separately, we discovered that the average general trust did *worse* than the Index in the first three years, better in the last two. Over periods covered by previous reports, we've found that the performance of the average general trust has not been very different from that of shares as a whole – sometimes better, sometimes worse.

The Consumers' Association did not claim to be testing the efficiency of the stock market, but that is what they were doing. Investment managers, stockbrokers and investment analysts are often uneasy with the suggestion that the market they serve is so efficient that they cannot consistently beat it. This seems to question their expertise, and to suggest that the costs they incur in becoming well-informed are a waste of money; but this is not the case. Information is worth pursuing so long as the marginal gain from its acquisition exceeds the marginal cost of acquisition. If expenditure stopped short of this point there would be extra profit to be earned by going further. When large numbers of market traders follow this rule they end up earning normal profits. In the stock market prices adjust to provide unbiased reflections of all information on risks and returns.

6 SUMMARY

- When large numbers of traders are found on each side of a market they are obliged to accept market prices as facts of life, determined by their joint behaviour, which they are individually too small to affect: suppliers and demanders are price-takers.
- In the short run suppliers who are price-takers seek to maximise quasi-rent, the contribution to non-variable costs. The best they can do may be to run at a loss.
- In the long run all costs must be covered. The output of individual firms and the number of firms adjusts until no one makes losses or abnormal profits.
- In long-run equilibrium, specialised factors in inelastic supply may be paid economic rent. Economic rent depends upon the level of product price, product price itself being determined by the interplay of long-run supply, which depends on costs excluding rent, and demand.
- In purely competitive markets, output is allocated efficiently between firms, economic rent determines the merit order in which factors are used, firms may be marginal because they are exceptionally productive elsewhere rather than inefficient in the market under consideration, bankruptcy may represent the re-valuation of assets and not their abandonment, and government policies intentionally or unintentionally are likely to end up benefiting rentiers.
- Good or bad business in a purely competitive market is a signal for firms to enter or leave, not a permanent state of affairs.

- The prosperity of a trade may be judged by its growth, stability or contraction.
- Perfect competition assumes a degree of knowledge possessed by market participants that is seldom found, but when it is, as in organised financial and commodity markets, prices adjust quickly to new information and fully reflect current knowledge.
- Market efficiency depends upon all the characteristics of perfect competition: freedom of entry of traders to take advantage of under-priced or over-priced commodities, large numbers so that no trader can dominate the market, homogeneous commodities that can be judged solely on price, and widespread knowledge of all market opportunities so that prices reflect all relevant knowledge.
- An efficient market may be recognised by the random walk of prices from day to day, by the speed of adjustment of prices to new information, and by inability of experts to consistently discover bargain prices.

6

MONOPOLY AND ECONOMIC WELFARE

1 INTRODUCTION

Monopoly must be regarded coolly. It may be good or bad, legitimate or illegitimate. There are three main reasons for pragmatism.

First, monopoly power has many sources. There are 'natural monopolies' in activities involving dedicated networks, such as water supply, or special locations, such as airports. Governments often play an active role in the creation of monopolies by nationalisation statutes, protective tariffs, and patent and copyright laws. Monopoly is sometimes the prize for outstanding success in competition, as monopolists often like to claim. On the other hand, it is also acquired by merger of rivals and conspiracy between erstwhile competitors.

Secondly, it is always a matter of degree. No single supplier or group acting together has complete sovereignty over the market. Customers can often do without or buy something else, there are often potential competitors lurking in the wings, and advances in technology make monopolised products obsolete.

Thirdly, the performance of monopolists is very mixed. Some make large profits and others modest profits or losses, some attain specially low costs and others incur unnecessarily high costs, and some are in the van of technological progress whilst others bring up the rear. The theory of monopoly must therefore encompass many possibilities.

The next section examines the equilibrium price and output of a monopolist charging the same price to all customers. The consequences for economic welfare are discussed in section 3. If customers charged high prices are unable to acquire goods from customers charged lower prices, it may be to a monopolist's advantage to vary prices with customers' circumstances. Section 4 is devoted to this possibility of price discrimination.

2 MONOPOLY EQUILIBRIUM

Pure monopoly is the opposite of pure competition: blocked entry instead of free entry to the market, one supplier instead of a large number of suppliers, and, as implied by there being only one supplier, a product that is completely different from all others. Some extreme cases, such as public utilities, tight cartels and firms owning basic patents, come close to satisfying these three conditions; but monopoly is usually a matter of degree.

The degree of monopoly

Various methods of measuring monopoly power have been put forward depending on the extent to which one or other of the conditions is satisfied. J.S. Bain suggested use of the ratio of the price at which new suppliers would enter the market to the competitive price that just covers normal profit. This would be a possible measure if entry always came from a new supplier whose costs could be estimated by accountants or engineers. However, entry often comes from established firms which cannot be identified in advance and which face lower costs than those of completely new suppliers.

R.W. Rothschild put forward an index that relied on the difference between demand as seen by a firm and market demand. The Rothschild index is the ratio of the slope of a firm's demand curve to the slope of the market demand curve. In pure monopoly the two curves coincide, giving an index of unity; in pure competition a firm's demand curve is horizontal, giving an index of zero; in between are various degrees of monopoly. Unfortunately, firms' demand curves are subjective and apart from monopoly and pure competition difficult for statisticians to measure.

A.P. Lerner confined attention to objective variables. His index measures:

$$\frac{\text{price} - \text{marginal cost}}{\text{price}}$$

In pure competition, price equals marginal cost, and the index is zero. This index relies on the degree of difference of the monopolist's product from that of others, or the closeness of substitutes, as it equals the inverse of the elasticity of demand.[1] However, the index might be low because costs are higher than need be and not because potential monopoly power is weak. The Lerner index draws attention to the fact that being the sole supplier may not be the means to unlimited riches.

Inequality of price and marginal cost

A pure monopolist enjoys the entire market for his speciality. He therefore has to take account of the entire market demand instead of being faced with a going market price. Whereas a pure competitor is a price-taker, a pure monopolist is a price-searcher: he must seek out his most profitable price. Mathematics does not change with market structure, so the condition for maximising profits, equating marginal costs with marginal receipts, remains unchanged. However, for a monopolist marginal revenue does not equal price: larger sales are associated with lower prices, and facing a falling demand curve the monopolist always finds marginal receipts less than average receipts, that is, less than price.

Three possible outcomes are depicted in Figure 6.1. In (a), marginal cost equals marginal receipts at output OA, which may be sold at price OC. At this price, total receipts OCDA exceed total cost (including normal profit) OBEA by an amount shown by the shaded rectangle BCDE. BCDE represents monopoly profit. This is the picture apt to come to mind when one thinks about monopoly. Hoffman-La Roche during the period of its tranquilliser patents, or OPEC at the peak of its power, fit this picture. Notice that when charging the same price to everyone, the monopolist may choose the most profitable output OA and accept the associated price OC, or may choose the most profitable price OC and accept the associated output OA. Output and price cannot be fixed independently.

In (b), the most profitable price and output yield no more than normal profit: marginal cost equals marginal receipts at the output at which average cost equals average receipts (the demand curve is tangential to the average costs curve at this output). This is a stylised picture of the situation found, for example, by the Monopolies Commission when it evaluated the profits of the London Brick Company, British Plasterboard, Pilkingtons, and Metal Box.

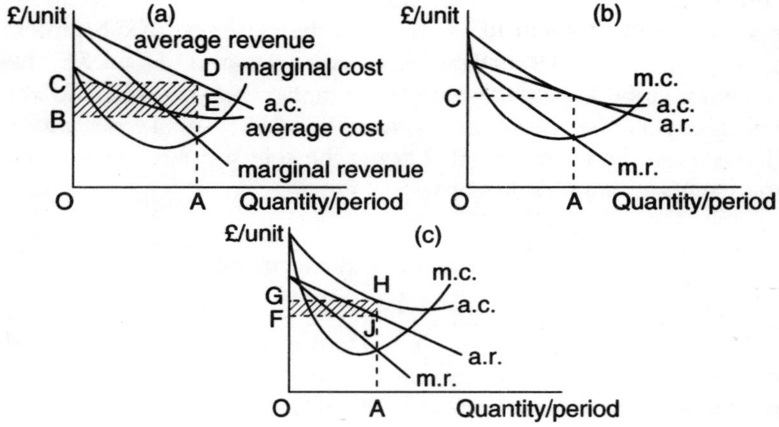

Figure 6.1 Profit maximising or loss minimising in three monopolies

The Commission found these companies no more than reasonably profitable.[2]

Figure 6.1(c) depicts the situation where a pure monopolist, charging all customers the same price, cannot even secure normal profits. Equating marginal costs with marginal receipts determines the smallest loss if production is undertaken; but, when marginal cost equals marginal receipts, average cost is greater than average receipts and a loss indicated by the rectangle FGHJ is incurred. (It will be seen later that it is sometimes possible for a monopolist to cover all costs including normal profit, despite the fact that average cost exceeds average revenue at all outputs, by price discrimination.) This third possibility may seem unrealistic, but it reproduces the situation that held for many years when the British Post Office was required to provide a telegram service. Innovators possessing patent monopolies often find themselves in this situation if their product fails to attract a big enough market; for example, Du Pont are said to have lost $100 million as the monopolist supplying the synthetic leather Corfam. A favourite monopoly, the Mersey Ferries, despite a unique product, find it difficult to cover costs.

Monopoly profits thus do not accrue automatically to monopolists. When they are available they provide an indicator of possible harm to economic welfare.

3 MONOPOLY AND ECONOMIC WELFARE

A recurrent problem in isolating the effects of economic arrangements is the need to make counterfactual comparisons. On the one hand is what is, and this must be compared with what might be. It is all too easy to imagine what might be as what one would like to be. In the case of monopoly, a simple model of a market supplied at constant average cost by a monopolist and, alternatively, by a number of identical competing firms points to some of the factors deserving investigation.

A simple model: income transfers, diverted production and dead-weight loss

Figure 6.2 illustrates the market. If it is supplied by competitive firms the quantity offered per period is OA, where the demand price OC equals average cost and marginal cost. If it is supplied by a monopolist the quantity offered per period is OB where marginal cost equals marginal revenue, and the price is OM. The monopoly price is higher, the quantity supplied smaller, and a monopoly profit of CMDE is received by the monopolist. From society's point

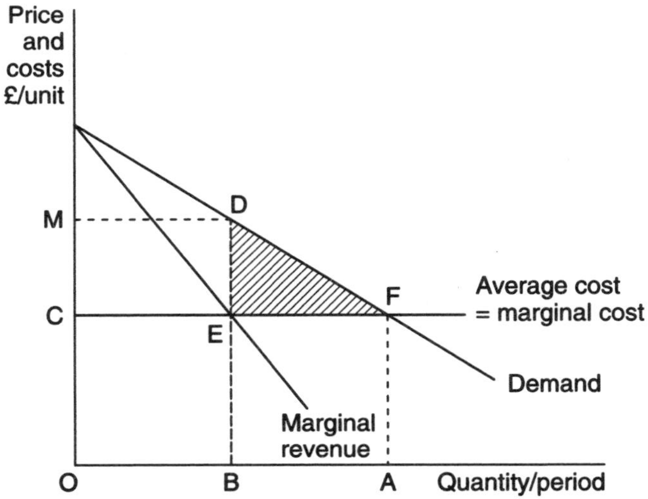

Figure 6.2 A simple model of competition and monopoly

of view, this may not be as serious as appears at first sight. There are three matters to consider.

First, provided that the monopoly is a domestic firm, the monopoly profit CMDE is a transfer of income from some members of the community to others. The recipients may be deserving or undeserving, and the contributors may be undeserving or deserving; but this is only one element in income distribution and, if the overall distribution of income is regarded as unsatisfactory, there are ample means for dealing with it. The significance of monopoly profit is different when the monopoly is a foreign one and the monopoly profit is transferred abroad. It is then a net loss to the community.

Secondly, consumers are deprived of the opportunity of spending BEFA on the good; but they can spend this sum elsewhere. Marginal cost is at the level shown because it reflects the value of inputs in other uses, that is, opportunity cost: consumers therefore gain elsewhere goods valued at BEFA.

However, given the chance, as in competitive conditions, they would have bought this product because it represented better value. This is the third point. Depriving consumers of the opportunity of buying BA at the competitive price deprives them of the extra value attached to the product, the consumers' surplus EDF. This is termed the 'dead-weight loss' because there is no offset. It arises because production of the monopolised product is too small and production of other goods too large, compared with the allocation of resources possible under competition.

OPEC and economic welfare

The simple model may be adapted to make a rough estimate of the effects of OPEC restrictions at the height of its power in the crude oil market: for this purpose we regard OPEC as a whole.[3] In 1970, before OPEC became a dominant force in the market, crude oil was priced $2.50 per barrel and OPEC countries sold 10 billion barrels. Forecasts at the time suggested that the rapid growth of demand and delays in developing new capacity would cause the price to double by 1980 to $5 per barrel, and OPEC production would also double to 20 billion barrels. In the event, OPEC production was held at 10 billion barrels but was sold at $30 per barrel: $30 and 10 billion barrels give one point on the 1980 demand curve, and, if the 1970 forecast is reliable, $5 and 20 billion barrels give another.

The difference made by OPEC is illustrated in Figure 6.3. In 1980, OPEC imposed a dead-weight loss on the world that can be valued at $125 billion, and transferred $250 billion into its coffers as monopoly profit. Membership of OPEC is a necessary and sufficient qualification for seeing merit in this outcome.[4] Fortunately it could not last.

Estimating dead-weight loss

OPEC members made the robber barons of old look like charity commissioners. Welfare costs of monopoly are not usually on such a scale. When the demand curve is linear and unit costs are constant, dead-weight loss may easily be calculated from monopoly profit. It equals half the monopoly profit. The marginal revenue curve bisects lines drawn at right-angles to the vertical axis, so, referring to Figure 6.2, EF = CE, and area EDF = 1/2(EF × ED) = 1/2(CE × ED), that is, equals one-half the monopoly profit. If the monopoly profit can be measured, measurement of dead-weight loss follows quickly.

In estimating monopoly profit care must be taken that all costs, including interest on owners' capital, are deducted from receipts,

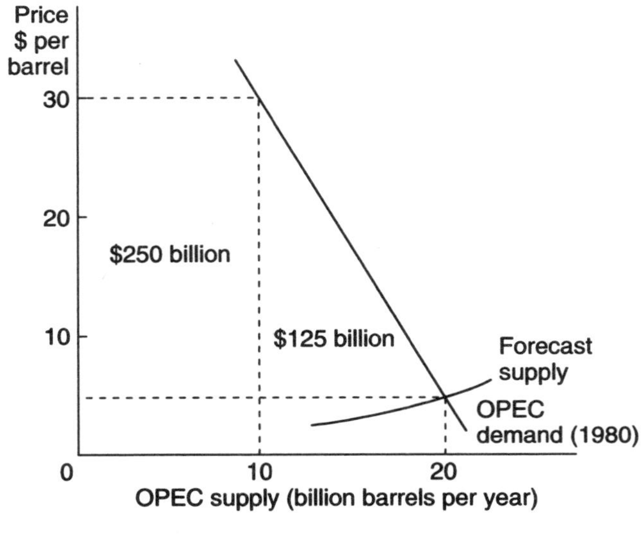

Figure 6.3 OPEC 1980

and that costs, such as depreciation, are properly calculated after making allowance for inflation. Account must then be taken of other possible sources of abnormal profits: disequilibrium in competitive markets, windfall gains, rewards for risk-taking and for innovation. Profits signalling disequilibrium or windfalls are easily identifiable in a run of profit figures because, by their nature, they are transitory. Rewards for risk-taking do not disappear but fluctuate with favourable and unfavourable contingencies: again they may be identified in a run of figures. Rewards for innovation are associated with a record of innovations undertaken. When all allowances are made, profits attributable to monopoly, and *a fortiori* dead-weight losses, are apt to shrink to modest proportions.

A second model: cost penalties and prizes

Something seems missing from such calculations, and something is. The effects of monopoly may be even smaller or much greater because costs may be lower or higher with monopoly than in competitive conditions. If concentration of production on a single supplier, sometimes described as rationalisation of production, results in lower costs, the effects are as in Figure 6.4. The diversion of production is less marked and the associated dead-weight loss is reduced, and there is a gain of HCKL representing the saving of resources absorbed in production. This gain accrues as monopoly profit, an income transfer, but it represents a real saving in resources. Furthermore, the reduced costs are enjoyed for all units produced: it is not a marginal matter of less consumption here and greater consumption there.

There is, however, a gloomier possibility. Monopolists have been known to proclaim the benefits of rationalised production attained by merging competitors whilst continuing to produce in the same old plants scattered about the country. They even may fail to keep costs down to their former level. Lacking the spur of competition costs may rise and may be incurred to satisfy staff rather than customers. The situation when monopoly results in higher costs is depicted in Figure 6.5.

Figure 6.5 shows a situation where monopoly profit has shrunk because of the higher level of unit costs, OR instead of OC; but this is no consolation because the reduced profits are associated with excessive quantities of inputs being used for each unit of output. Total output contracts because of the high level of costs, and the

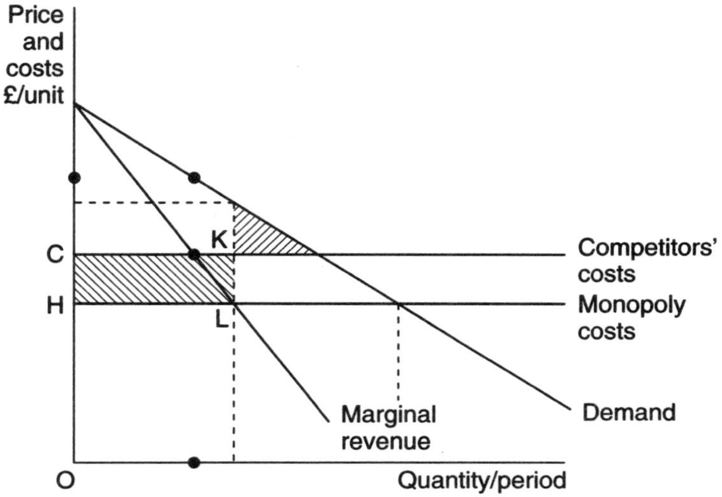

Figure 6.4 Monopoly with cost advantage

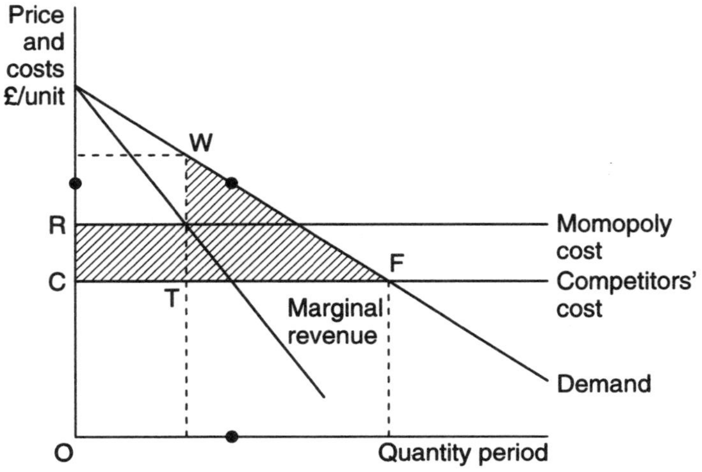

Figure 6.5 Monopoly with excessive costs

diversion of demand involves a bigger dead-weight loss of TWF.

The diversion of resources from monopolised to competitive sectors may sometimes be reduced or eliminated by price discrimination; but greater transfers of income from consumers to suppliers are involved. Price discrimination may also make possible provision of goods, without subsidy, when receipts would not cover costs at any single price. In other cases price discrimination is a means to increased profit at the expense of consumers.

4 PRICE DISCRIMINATION

Price discrimination consists of charging different prices for different units of production although costs are identical for all units, charging the same price for different units although they have involved different costs (for example, different delivery costs or credit terms), or charging different prices for different units that do not correspond to any differences in costs: charging different prices with identical costs, identical prices with different costs, or different prices not corresponding to cost differences. In general terms, prices of different units bear differing ratios to marginal costs – P_1:MC ≠ P_2:MC . . . .

Necessary conditions

Two conditions must be satisfied for price discrimination to be possible: first, supply must be controlled by a monopoly so that high prices cannot be undercut by competitors; and, secondly, customers must be unable to trade with one another so that those enjoying low prices cannot resell to those charged higher prices. There is a third condition that must be satisfied if price discrimination between segments of markets is to be profitable: elasticities of demand for segments must differ at sales volumes at which marginal cost equals marginal receipts.

Types of discrimination

A.C. Pigou distinguished three degrees of price discrimination. The first two refer to treatment of individual consumers, and the third to treatment of groups of consumers. First-degree discrimination, sometimes termed 'perfect discrimination' because price distinctions can be carried no further, involves charging a customer a different price for each unit bought. Second-degree discrimination involves charging lower prices for successive batches. Third-degree discrimination involves varying prices to match differing strengths of demand of different groups of consumers.

First degree discrimination

Consider the demand of an individual consumer such as that illustrated in Figure 6.6. Provided that the good takes up only a small part of income, so that income effects may be ignored, the demand curve may be interpreted as showing that this individual would pay OP_1 for one unit of the good rather than go without, would pay OP_2 for a second unit, OP_3 for a third unit, and so on.[5] A monopolist who varied his price in this systematic fashion, unit by unit, would be engaging in first-degree discrimination. He would continue to offer successive units at lower prices until the price reached the level of marginal cost: up to this point each unit sold adds to profits.

Ability to discriminate in this fashion presupposes very detailed knowledge of the market. Haggling in Eastern bazaars may be thought of as a process of discovering such information; but the

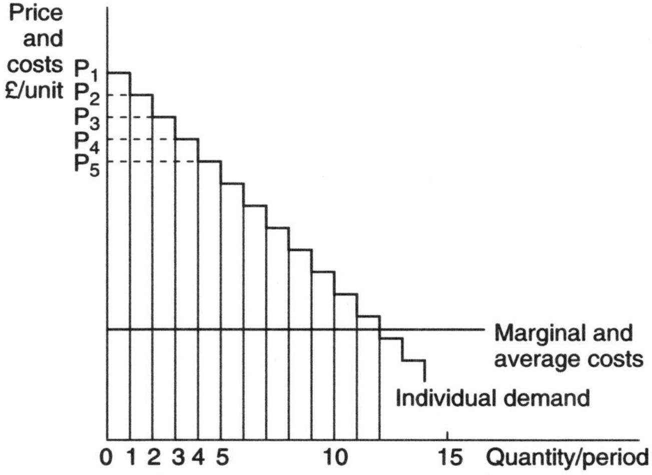

Figure 6.6 First-degree price discrimination

bilateral nature of such bargaining does not lead to a pre-determined outcome, and sellers in bazaars are seldom monopolists. It has been suggested that IBM, in the early post-war years when it dominated main-frame computers, attained a fine degree of discrimination between its customers by requiring them to pay for computer services in two parts, a computer rent plus a charge per punched card used to feed in input that was well in excess of the cost of the cards. The total charge automatically required users to pay more for extra use of their computers.

It may be possible to come near to first-degree discrimination by offering all-or-nothing contracts. Instead of being offered the schedule of prices depicted in Figure 6.6, a customer may be offered, as in Figure 6.7, the choice of OA at price ON or nothing at all. In the case illustrated it is just worth while making the purchase as the consumer's surplus on the early units OB just offsets the payments in excess of demand prices on units BA. This may seem a fanciful suggestion, but wholesale buyers of diamonds from De Beers Central Selling Organisation are offered parcels of diamonds at an inclusive price and the parcels must be bought as a whole. There may be some first-degree price discrimination in this arrangement.[6] All-or-nothing contracts are also offered by some theme parks that charge for admission but then provide rides 'free'.

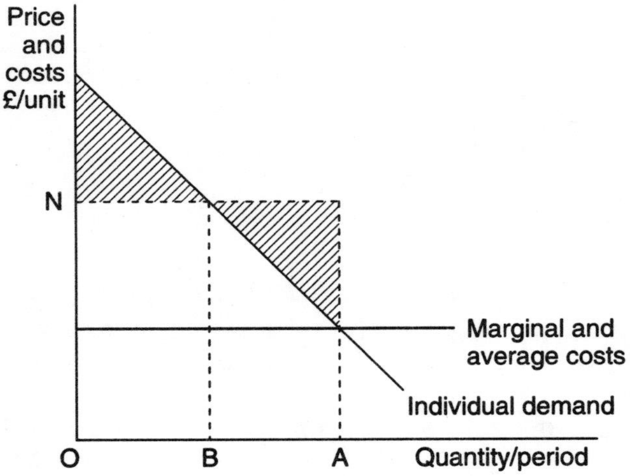

Figure 6.7 All-or-nothing contract

Distant approaches to first-degree discrimination may be found in some popular marketing ploys. For example, the offer of one tube of toothpaste for 75p and two for £1.25 is equivalent to a price of 75p for the first tube and 50p for the second.

A notable feature of first-degree discrimination is that it involves no restriction of output by a monopolist. Marginal revenue is provided by successive demand prices, and a profit-maximising monopolist equating marginal cost with marginal receipts at the same time equates marginal cost with demand price. This is equivalent to the outcome in a competitive market so far as the level of output and allocation of resources are concerned. There is, of course, the major difference that the value of consumer's surplus is transferred in its entirety to the monopolist as monopoly profit.

Second-degree discrimination

Second-degree discrimination is less precise than first-degree discrimination. Instead of price varying for each successive unit, price varies with successive blocks of units purchased. For example, electricity tariffs have sometimes imposed a high charge per unit on a first block of units purchased and lower charges on subsequent blocks. The discount terms offered in some wholesale price-lists carry such distinctions to considerable length.

Block tariffs and quantity discounts cannot be identified as second-degree discrimination without further investigation. When electricity was first introduced the peak load was for lighting, and a high charge for a first block of units was a means of varying charges on-peak and off-peak. Quantity discounts may reflect economies of long runs of production and savings in clerical work and delivery costs.

Third-degree discrimination

The most common form of price discrimination is third-degree discrimination, where the market is segmented and different groups of consumers are offered different prices, consumers with inelastic demand being obliged to pay a higher price than those with elastic demand. Examples are full fares paid by businessmen and concessionary fares paid by students and senior citizens on the railways, prices charged to private motorists for replacement car parts and to car manufacturers for initial equipment, hairdressers' charges for teenagers (marketers define teenage as 16–24) and pensioners, and prices for a wide range of goods at home and abroad or in rich and poor districts. The mechanics of third-degree discrimination are illustrated in Figure 6.8.

In Figure 6.8 a market is divided into two sections (a) and (b), with demand more elastic in (b) than in (a) at each price. The marginal revenue curves in (a) and (b) are added horizontally to produce the combined marginal revenue curve in (c). Equating marginal cost with combined marginal revenue determines the most profitable output OC, and this is divided to supply OA at price OP_1 in (a) and OB at price OP_2 in (b). It may be seen that marginal revenue is the same in each market segment so there would be no advantage in switching sales between segments, and marginal cost equals marginal revenue so there would be no advantage in choosing a different rate of output.

Third-degree discrimination may make possible the supply of goods when no single price exists at which receipts would cover costs. Academic journals often provide examples. The purchasers

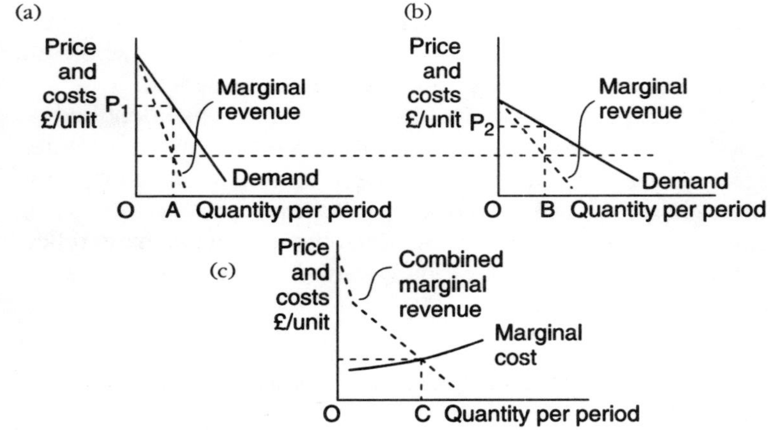

Figure 6.8 Third-degree discrimination
(a) Market with less-elastic demand: e.g. business travel, replacement parts, teenage hairstyling, domestic markets, rich areas
(b) Market with more-elastic demand: e.g. student travel, initial equipment, pensioners' haircuts, foreign markets, poor areas
(c) Combined market

of such journals fall into two groups, libraries and independent scholars. Libraries have few substitutes for books and journals, and so library demand is inelastic. Scholars are impelled by narrowness of purse and breadth of interests to be responsive to varying prices. The resulting situation for a typical journal is illustrated in Figure 6.9. The library demand is LL_1, the scholars demand SS_1, and the combined demand, obtained by adding the two demand curves horizontally, is LTT_1. The combined demand curve lies below average total costs along its entire length, in other words there is no single price at which receipts would cover costs. However, 500 libraries are prepared to pay £40 per year, and 1,000 scholars are prepared to pay £17.50 per year. If these subscription rates are offered, the average subscription will be £25 which is just sufficient to cover average costs for a circulation of 1,500.

Publishers and authors have been known to argue on similar lines when justifying the difference in price between hard-back and paper-back books. Book pricing is an example of price discrimination where different prices are charged for goods involving different costs but where the differences in prices are not in proportion to the differences in costs. It would be easier to accept such pricing as a civilised response to the cruelties of the

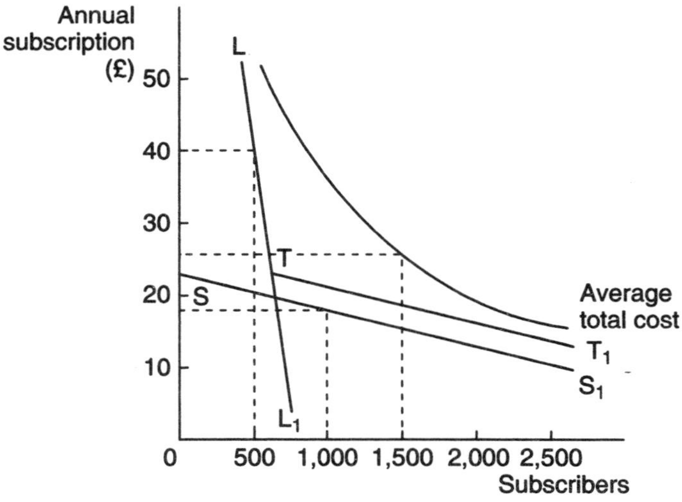

Figure 6.9 Supply made possible by price discrimination

market-place if authors, paid a percentage of total receipts, did not have such a clear interest in maximising total revenue, and publishers, who after all must live, did not have such a clear interest in the somewhat smaller total revenue at which profits are maximised.[7]

5 SUMMARY

- The condition for profit maximisation, marginal cost equals marginal revenue, is the same for a monopoly as for any other kind of firm; but, except in the case of first-degree discrimination, price is greater than marginal revenue because a monopolist faces a downward-sloping market demand curve.
- Monopolised markets may offer opportunities for supernormal, normal or subnormal profits depending upon the strength of demand and level of costs.
- In a monopolised market output is lower and price higher than would be the case if competition were active. Monopoly thus diverts resources from their most valued use and imposes a dead-weight loss. Monopoly profit is an income transfer which is a net loss to the community only when transferred abroad.
- The dead-weight loss may be roughly estimated as one-half of the monopoly profit. In estimating monopoly profit care must be taken to account for all costs and to exclude disequilibrium and windfall profits, rewards for risk-taking and for innovation.
- The burden imposed by monopoly may be lightened if concentration of production reduces costs or be made heavier if monopoly protects inefficiency.
- Monopolists may be able to separate transactions and offer a range of prices instead of a single price. First-degree discrimination involves charging individual customers different prices for successive units bought: all-or-nothing contracts may offer an alternative means to this end. Second-degree discrimination involves charging different prices for successive blocks purchased. Third-degree discrimination involves charging different prices to groups of customers classified according to elasticity of demand.
- As with other forms of monopoly behaviour, price discrimination may be good or bad depending upon circumstances: it may make possible supplies of goods that could not be made available at a single price.

- Monopoly theory provides a guide to features to look out for when analysing and evaluating monopolies. It points towards pragmatism rather than dogmatism: towards the British Monopolies Commission rather than US anti-trust agencies.

7

OLIGOPOLY: INTERDEPENDENT DECISIONS

1 INTRODUCTION

It will be recalled that in *The Final Problem* Sherlock Holmes is pursued and attacked by Professor Moriarty and his agents who are intent on murdering Holmes before he can secure their arrest and conviction. He just eludes Moriarty at Victoria Station when the train pulls out in the nick of time. Holmes rightly calculates that his pursuer will do the same as he would in the circumstances and engage a special train in order to overtake the regular train at Dover. Holmes and Watson therefore alight at Canterbury and watch Moriarty speed past before making their way across country to Newhaven. Holmes hints at the complexity of his thought processes by pointing out that Moriarty might have deduced what he had deduced and in a master-stroke have chartered his special train no further than Canterbury. Holmes is sure that Moriarty will not do this. If Holmes had deduced that Moriarty would deduce that he would get off at Canterbury then Holmes and Watson would themselves have continued to Dover; but Moriarty might allow for this and go straight to Dover after all, which if Holmes foresaw . . . The Holmes–Moriarty problem is one of interdependent decision-making.[1]

Conscious interdependence of decisions of rival suppliers is the characteristic feature of oligopoly, and it raises as many 'if–but problems' of theory and practice as Holmes at his most devious. The next section surveys some early theories. Section 3 is devoted to the application of the theory of games. Section 4 examines the problems faced when firms seek to escape from the uncertainties of interdependent decisions by tacit collusion, pursuing joint instead of single profit maximisation or adopting one of their number as price-leader. Open collusion in cartels is limited by domestic and EC laws; but in any case cartels have inherent weaknesses. Section 5 looks at the conflicting forces at work within cartels such as OPEC. Secton 6 is devoted to the role rules of thumb may play in oligopolistic and monopolistic markets.

2 SOME EARLY THEORIES

Cournot

The earliest theorist in this area was A.A. Cournot who examined the behaviour of duopolists with identical constant costs (simplified to zero average costs), producing a homogeneous product, natural mineral water. If they were to collude to maximise joint profit, output would be restricted to the point where marginal receipts equalled marginal cost, and the two would somehow have to agree shares of the monopoly output. If they were to ignore each other they would continue to expand output so long as price exceeded average cost, total output would be the same as with pure competition but, with identical constant costs, its allocation between the two would be indeterminate. Cornot analysed a third possibility: that each duopolist, when deciding output, assumes the rival's output is fixed. This leaves each duopolist with a residual demand curve and the ability to produce where residual marginal revenue equals marginal cost. As they proceed in this fashion they must eventually reach an equilibrium where each faces an identical residual demand, and the best each can do is to continue with the associated output. The sum of their outputs exceeds the monopoly output but is less than the purely competitive output.

Cornot's model is instructive in two respects. First, despite interdependent decision-making, compatible rates of output are reached without any collusion. The equilibrium is of a special kind: each duopolist does the best he can in the correct belief that his rival is doing the best he can and thus neither has any incentive to make further changes. This kind of equilibrium, dependent on the correct estimation of the situation and behaviour of identifiable competitors, has come to be known as a Nash equilibrium, following its introduction into games theory by John Nash. Secondly, it draws attention to the possibility that the outcome in an oligopolistic market may lie somewhere between the extremes of monopoly and pure competition.

Bertrand

A solution at the competitive extreme was introduced by J. Bertrand with duopolists deciding their prices on the assumption that rival price, rather than output, is fixed. On this assumption, the whole market seems available by undercutting the rival price until price is forced down to the competitive level. The Bertrand model is worth keeping in mind as a reminder that two is a sufficient number for active competition and that oligopoly may not be as sinister as it sounds.

Edgeworth

The Cournot and Bertrand assumptions are difficult to swallow because they involve beliefs about rival behaviour that are bound to be disproved except at the Nash equilibrium. F.Y. Edgeworth introduced a simple modification which has surprising results. What would happen if duopolists have limited capacity and could not separately satisfy the entire market? If they begin with the monopoly output permitting joint profit maximisation, it would be possible for one duopolist to fill his entire capacity by slightly shading the price, but because what is good for one is good for the other, price would be competed down until both produce at capacity. At this point, it becomes worth while to look at the residual demand available when a rival can take no more of the market: a price increase appears profitable. In the Edgeworth model price fluctuates up and down. This provides some theoretical support for the defence frequently offered by oligopolists accused of restricting competition, that they seek to avoid instability, not competition.

There is some evidence that prices fluctuate more in oligopolistic than monopolistic markets, for example, in markets for different kinds of ethical drugs, markets for advertising in monopolistic and oligopolistic trade journals, and communities with one or two utility companies. However, there is also evidence, open to conflicting interpretations, of rigid prices. In the twenty-five years of full employment following the Second World War one of the most frequent criticisms of British manufacturers was their long delivery times: they were evidently not setting market-clearing prices. D.W. Carlton examined how often price changes once it has been set for an individual buyer, finding prices remaining unchanged for about eighteen months in steel, chemicals and cement.[2] A possible explanation of rigid prices is provided by the kinked demand model introduced by P.M. Sweezy.

Kinked demand

A kinked demand curve is a construction incorporating objective commercial facts and subjective estimates of demand in the light of assumed behaviour of rivals. The starting point is a market-share demand curve representing sales opportunities facing a single oligopolist when his fellows charge prices identical with his own. It may be combined with subjective demand estimates of likely sales if a firm unilaterally changes price. For example, in Figure 7.1(a), a firm's market share demand curve is given by DD_1: the market price is OB and the firm's share of sales OA. The firm might believe that, provided rivals continued to charge OB, sales could be attained along the more elastic subjective demand curve dd_1.

This would be optimistic. A realist might accept the upper part of dd_1, reckoning that rivals would willingly see him lose sales; but if he reduced price others would be forced to follow and sales would only increase by amounts shown on the lower branch of DD_1. This produces the composite demand curve dCD_1 of Figure 7.1(b), with an outward kink at the ruling market price. At this price marginal revenue is undefined because of the discontinuity in the rate of change of total revenue. There is a marginal revenue curve corresponding to each wing of the demand curve, but a gap

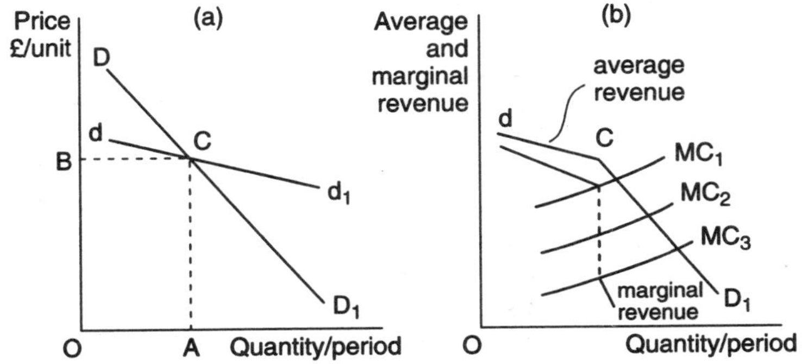

Figure 7.1 Kinked demand

between the two. The gap means that costs could fluctuate a good deal yet the most profitable price remain the going price.

Objections are sometimes raised because this model begins with a historic price, rather than explaining this price; but a beginning has to be made somewhere. A more substantial objection is that kinked demand curves are of little help in explaining what will happen if market innovations occur or costs shift beyond the limits of the gap in marginal revenue. Kinked demand curves may have something to offer in placid periods but they fail in more exciting times.

There are other, more mundane, reasons why oligopolists may avoid frequent price changes. Costs are incurred preparing, announcing and circulating new price lists and discount terms. There is the danger that if prices are cut they may be seen by competitors as the declaration of a price war. Competitors may not wish to meet a price cut but they require no special skill to make a cut of their own. Alternative strategies are therefore attractive. Product improvement is more difficult to copy, and many of the most innovative firms with the largest research departments, such as chemical and pharmaceutical manufacturers, are found in oligopolistic markets. Oligopolists are also amongst the heaviest spenders on marketing and advertising. Game theory may throw some light on such spending.

3 GAME THEORY

Game theory provides general methods for analysing interdependent decision-making from draughts and poker to politics and military strategy. Games differ in hostility, the most aggressive being zero-sum games where winnings equal losses. Competition for market-share is a zero-sum game; but such games are not common in economics, because production and exchange add value so that all may gain, or, if costs are enhanced, all may lose. They also differ in the extent to which information is common to all players, whether players may co-operate with binding agreements, the number of players, the sequence of play and the number of times games are played. This section is devoted to a non-zero-sum, non-co-operative game between two players which has many applications, the prisoners' dilemma game.[3]

In game theory a game consists of individuals or groups (known as players) who obey a set of rules stipulating starting conditions, legal moves which may be simultaneous or in a specified order, and the terms of the outcome or payoff. In the present case players are firms and payoffs are profits.

An advertising game

Consider two detergent manufacturers, L and G, each independently deciding whether to add £1 million to the advertising budget. The matrix of pay-offs, putting L's gains or losses top-right and G's bottom left is shown in Figure 7.2(a). It takes the form of a prisoners' dilemma game. If both leave their budgets unchanged, they will both be better off by £1 million saved. If G leaves his budget unchanged and L increases his, L will gain £1.5 million and G lose £1.5 million. Similarly, if L leaves his budget unchanged and G increases his, G will gain £1.5 million and L lose £1.5 million. If both increase expenditure by £1 million, both will be out of pocket by £1 million: the additional advertising of one simply offsetting the additional advertising of the other.

In these circumstances, if G leaves his budget unchanged, the best L can do is to increase his advertising and enjoy a payoff of £1.5 million. If G increases his expenditure by £1 million, the best L can do is still to increase his advertising: he will be worse off by £1 million, but he would be worse off by £1.5 million if he kept his advertising constant. The increase strategy dominates and must be followed. The same argument applies to G. Both manufacturers

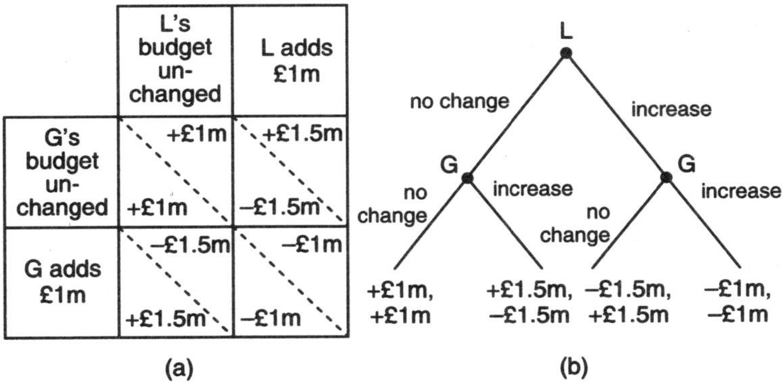

Figure 7.2 An advertising dilemma

deciding expenditure on their own are forced to decisions that waste resources in offsetting advertising.

Notice that this outcome results from the structure of the game and not from the players being ignorant of each other's moves. Figure 7.2(a) sets out the game in normal form; 7.2(b) sets out the game in extensive form, as seen by G, with L going first. In the pairs of payoffs, G's are given first. G inevitably increases expenditure. It is not a matter of ignorance, although the structure of the game excludes ignorance. Ignorance would be depicted in the extensive form by drawing a boundary of ignorance around L_1 and L_2. G's decision would be unchanged. Furthermore, it would do no good if L promised to maintain his budget; G would have no reason to believe him, and following the rules L would break his promise. The players cannot make convincing commitments.

This possibility of mutually offsetting advertising is not a fanciful one. In early post-war years, before such agreements became subject to the jurisdiction of the Restrictive Practices Court, Unilever and Proctor & Gamble made an agreement to limit their expenditure to the level of the previous twelve months. The agreement broke down because the two companies could not agree on the treatment of the advertising of new products, but the incentive to make it was a joint wish to avoid wasteful advertising expenditures.

However, without formal agreements, detergent manufacturers do not force each other into ever-increasing advertising expenditures. The game as presented had the special feature of being a one-shot game, whereas detergent sales go on from year to year. In a game that goes on indefinitely the payoffs are the present value of alternative strategies, and the highest present value attaches to mutual restraint. When players are faced with the same prisoners' dilemma game again and again they must come to recognise where their joint interest lies. A whole range of possible strategies have been tested by computer simulations and most eventually settle on the best joint choice. It has been found that an unaggressive tit-for-tat strategy converges most quickly on the best solution. In the detergent example the best strategy is to begin with an unchanged advertising budget, and if the rival also maintains his budget then leave it that way; if the rival increases his expenditure do the same, continue to retaliate but immediately respond in the same direction to a reduction in expenditure.[4]

Game theory suggests that Adam Smith's invisible hand may not always be providential. His aphorism about business merrymaking may also be questioned.

4 TACIT COLLUSION

As Smith would have it: 'People of the same trade seldom meet together, even for merriment and diversion, but the conversation ends in a conspiracy against the public, or in some contrivance to raise prices.'[5] It is true that, if entry of new suppliers is barred, existing competitors can always improve their lot by avoiding competition, but in doing so they create the conditions in which any one of them may improve his lot by renewing competition. If conspiracy is to be more than idle talk, agreement must be codified, monitored and enforced. This cannot be easily achieved when open agreements are outlawed and collusion must be tacit rather than explicit.

Parallel pricing

When there is no potential competition from possible newcomers, joint profit maximisation might seem the most likely outcome of competition between a few suppliers. They must be aware that the welfare of each depends upon the restraint of others, and this could result in mutual self-restraint. The Monopolies Commission argued that this was the case, for example, with producers of breakfast cereals: 'about 90 per cent of the market is in the hands of three manufacturers. With so few manufacturers competing, the pricing tactics of any one of them would be bound to affect the market shares of the others . . . Thus the manufacturers would see the result of price competition as a lower general level of prices with no competitive advantage to any of them.'[6] It is not always easy to determine whether parallel behaviour is tacit collusion aimed at joint profit maximisation or uniform response of rivals to uniform changes in costs or demand conditions.

Price leadership

The same ambiguity confronts judgement of price leadership where one firm customarily initiates price changes and others follow suit. This may be no more than a temporal pattern of prices, or it may be a tacit conspiracy to limit output in order to raise prices and profits. Four models of price leadership are of interest: low cost leadership, barometric leadership, monopolistic leadership and dominant firm leadership. In all cases leadership may be identified when one firm is always followed by rivals when it raises its prices: following price reductions is not a matter of choice but is imposed by competition.

Low-cost leadership

There may be little freedom of choice about following a low-cost leader if more intense competition is to be avoided. When the costs of oligopolists differ they may all gain by abstaining from price competition, but the most profitable price level will vary from firm to firm. Figure 7.3 illustrates the situation of three oligopolists with equal market shares but differing costs. Firms B and C would prefer higher prices than A but must perforce accept A's profit-maximising price OA as an upper limit.

J.A. Guthrie gave an explanation of low-cost leadership to a US Congress committee investigating newsprint, where International Paper acted as price leader:

> A businessman is in business to make a profit. The going price is the best he can get because his competitors are

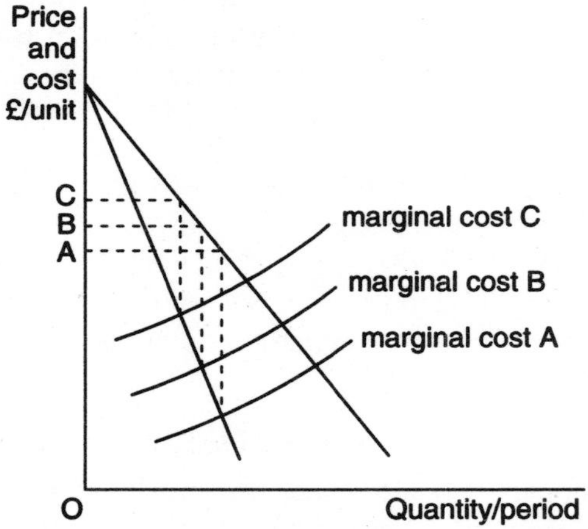

Figure 7.3 Low costs rule

> charging that figure. And even though his costs are higher than theirs and he would like to charge more, he cannot do so. On the other hand, he does not want to charge less than they do because his costs are higher than theirs. International Paper, in my opinion, has been a low cost company. Those firms that have higher costs cannot charge higher prices and they certainly do not want to take lower prices.[7]

Low-cost leadership seems a valid model so long as the firms determine their prices independently. When interdependence is recognised, the outcome becomes less certain. A and B might calculate that C's preferred price is the highest they could attain: their subjective demand curves would then have a horizontal section at price OC, and the kinked demand might indicate OC as the profit-maximising price for all three oligopolists.

Barometric leadership

A low-cost leader only finds advantage in changing prices when demand or cost conditions change, and such a firm could be regarded as providing barometric readings of the market. Firms experiencing similar cost and demand conditions might also regard one of their number, say the oldest, as a barometer. For the first six decades of this century steel prices in America were noted for their uniformity as a result of all companies accepting US Steel as price leader. G.M. Humphrey, chairman of National Steel, explained to the Kefauver Senate Committee his company's policy of following US Steel's price increases: 'I would think that [if the leader raises his prices] there would be some very good reason for his doing so . . . It would mean that something had happened that required a substantial increase in price.'[8]

Barometric price leadership has been seen as no more than the institutional form taken by price competition when small numbers of rivals are faced with the dangers of instability in interdependent decision-making. This could be the case; but equally the price barometer could continually register the monopoly price. National Steel's explanation provoked the comment by Senator Kefauver: 'As I interpret that, Mr Humphrey, you would be ashamed of yourself if you did not get what the traffic would bear.'

Monopolistic leadership

The simplest form of monopolistic price leadership would be for the leader to estimate the monopoly price and the rest to follow; but this requires a very knowledgeable leader. A monopoly price might be approximated by the highest-cost producer being allowed to lead. This was the Monopolies Commission's opinion of the UK salt market which is in effect a duopoly with ICI and British Salt having a combined market share of 95 per cent. British Salt is the low-cost producer but was found to follow ICI in its pricing. The Commission commented that British Salt believed that if they 'sought to undercut ICI this would have provoked a damaging retaliation'. However, the Commission concluded: 'We do not accept that these reasons demonstrate the existence of a competitive market. If anything they merely serve to show the lack of effective competition by a company well placed to offer it.'[9]

Dominant firm leadership

The danger of interdependent pricing degenerating into price war is often pointed to in justification of tacit collusion. As Judge Elbert H. Gary put it at one of his famous dinners for fellow steel manufacturers, companies should follow United's prices in order 'to maintain to a reasonable extent the equilibrium of business, to prevent utter demoralisation of business and destructive competition'.[10] In Judge Gary's reign United Steel had 65 per cent of the American market; fifty years later the total market had greatly expanded but United's share had dwindled to 25 per cent. There may be a moral in this for dominant price leaders.

The analysis of a market consisting of a dominant firm together with a fringe of smaller competitors is of special interest as it may combine monopolistic decisions of the dominant firm, tolerating free supplies from the fringe, together with competitive decisions by the remaining firms to supply as much as they wish at the leader's price. The situation is illustrated in Figure 7.4. $DFHD_1$ represents demand in the market as a whole. If the dominant firm deducts quantities expected to be supplied by the fringe from the total quantity demanded at each price, it obtains its individual demand curve $LEHD_1$. The fringe of small firms, accepting the price chosen by the dominant firm, act as price-takers in a similar way to pure competitors, each supplying the quantity at which marginal

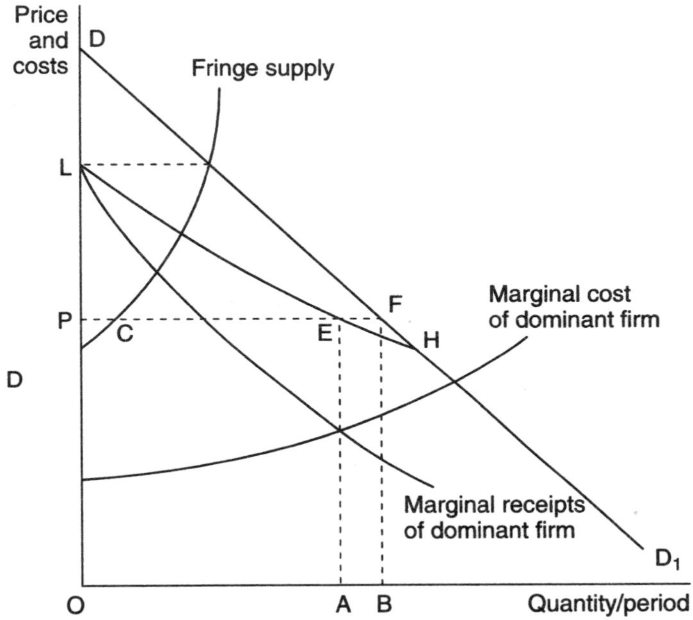

Figure 7.4 Dominant firm price leadership

cost equals price. The price leader enjoys maximum profits at the output at which his marginal cost equals the marginal revenue associated with his residual demand. In his case marginal revenue does not equal price because it reflects both total market demand and fringe supply. The most profitable output for the dominant firm is OA which sells at price OP, supplies of PC (= EF) coming from the fringe to make a total quantity supplied of OB.

Dominant firm leadership is possibly a misnomer: it could be termed 'accommodating leadership' because the leader has to make room for competitors' supplies. A double application of the dominant price leader model is used in the next section to explain the pricing of oil in the 1970s and 1980s when the market was dominated by OPEC and OPEC was dominated by Saudi Arabia.

5 OPEN COLLUSION: CARTELS

A cartel is an association formed to control supplies reaching the market. It may cover any or all of the following activities: price-fixing, output-limitation, removal of old capacity or investment in new plant, market-sharing, joint-selling, cross-licensing of patents and exchange of know-how, and profit-pooling. When most of these activities are covered a cartel is a separate unit of decision-making to which the theory of monopoly applies. For example, the classic cartels of Imperial Germany, such as the Rhenish–Westphalian Coal Cartel, were in much the same position as their members would have been had they merged their companies into a single undertaking. Joint profit maximisation rules. In recent years cartels have usually been looser organisations constituting variants of oligopolistic markets.

Agreeing and complying

There is usually a political element in the history of cartels. Cartels need the acquiescence of the law as in pre-war Britain, the protection of the law as in pre-war Germany, conflicts of sovereignty as in shipping, or the active intervention of government as in the formation of marketing boards. They incorporate the same basic conflict of interests as in tacit collusion. Cartel agreements are made to enhance profits, but extra profit invites extra competition. Monopoly profits attract new suppliers and so means are required to exclude new entrants. In addition members can improve their individual profits if they can find means to increase their share of the market at the monopoly price. They cannot all increase market-share, however, and the cartel may break apart. An increased market-share may be sought by methods which increase costs, such as increased advertising or improved quality, or by surreptitiously cutting prices: in the first case monopoly profit is eroded and in the second the cartel is undermined.

Cartels may channel market forces but they cannot abolish them. Prices and terms of trading must be agreed, and, as agreements are not usually self-enforcing, there needs to be some means of policing compliance. Agreement is more easily reached the fewer the negotiators, the simpler the definition of markets, and the more obvious any breach of the terms. Chemical manufacturers have strong incentives to reach a *modus vivendi* with one another. They need to co-ordinate plans for investment in large-scale plant if they are to avoid recurrent excess capacity. High fixed costs and low variable costs make the outbreak of a price war seem particularly ominous. Chemical manufacturers are in frequent contact because of patent exchange agreements. Markets may be allocated on a geographical basis. It is no surprise, therefore, that some of the most progressive companies, such as ICI and Shell, should have found themselves at odds with the European Commission over the pricing of major innovations, such as polypropylene, PVC and plastic film.

Efficiency

J.A. Schumpeter and J.K. Galbraith both drew attention to the fact that it is often the same firms that find themselves facing criticism for their marketing methods and praise for their technological leadership.[11] Cartels and economic efficiency do not always go together. The agreements require the consent of the firms with the highest costs, and so cartels may provide a shelter for inefficiency. This was the main criticism of the so-called reconstruction cartels of the 1930s. Promotion of inefficiency has also been seen in more recent years. Until the mid-1980s scheduled airlines made up one of the strongest international cartels, the International Air Transport Association (IATA). It had the backing of governments that owned the majority of national airlines and that would only give landing rights on condition that IATA rates were observed. Yet most airlines made little if any profits and became bywords for overmanning, expensive sales promotion and a rapid procession of new aircraft types.

Institutionalised price leadership

The other major international cartel, OPEC, has different lessons to offer. OPEC is riven by a remarkable number of divisions of interest and ambition,[12] yet it maintained its grip on the price of crude oil for more than a decade. This was partly fortuitous: open warfare between two members, Iran and Iraq, kept two million barrels per year off the market; but it was mainly because of the disproportionate economic power of Saudi Arabia. Saudi Arabia has shut-in capacity greater than the output of the rest of OPEC. This huge capacity is also extremely low-cost capacity, oil being drawn from near the surface under natural pressure. The main component of Saudi cost is user cost, that is, the present value of future revenue forgone if oil is sold immediately. Saudi Arabia could call the tune. In the late 1970s it had difficulty spending or safely investing its oil revenues and so was a congenial partner for countries facing greater sacrifices should they forgo immediate production.

OPEC has never encompassed all world production. In 1973, when OPEC contrived the first big increase in the price of crude, member states were responsible for 65 per cent of non-communist production, and their share has dwindled as OPEC prices attracted resources into exploration and production. OPEC has behaved in a similar way to a dominant price-leader: the cartel has been content to allow outsiders to provide whatever crude oil they wished at the OPEC price. OPEC demand equals world demand minus the quantities offered at alternative prices by outsiders. For the first ten years, Saudi Arabia was content to restrict its output to the extent necessary to accommodate supplies from other members. Within OPEC, Saudi demand equalled OPEC demand minus outputs agreed by other members. In choosing its output Saudi Arabia acted in effect as a dominant firm price-leader.

Uncontrolled entry

Saudi dominance simplified the problem of securing agreement on output quotas, and reduced the problem of monitoring and enforcing agreement to small proportions. However, the situation could only continue so long as Saudi Arabia was prepared to cut production. In 1984, OPEC accounted for 42 per cent of crude output and had cut production from 11.3 billion barrels to 6.3 billion. In the meantime output of non-OPEC producers rose from 6.2 to 8.9 billion barrels to account for 58 per cent of the total. In 1973, production in the UK was tiny, but in 1984 UK production exceeded that of every OPEC member except Saudi Arabia. Mexico had become an even larger producer. Over time the OPEC demand curve shifted to the left and the Saudi residual demand shifted to the left. In the mid-1980s Saudi Arabia saw its revenue contract and argued that all members should share restrictions on output. There have been few clearer examples of the importance of the entry of new suppliers undermining monopoly power.

Furthermore, as production quotas tightened, observance of agreements weakened. Lloyds of London were commissioned to report on oil movements, but surreptitious price-cuts became more frequent. Oil has been sold together with tanker freightage at low rates, generous credit terms have been offered, refineries financed at low cost, loans made to customers at low rates of interest, oil bartered on favourable terms for armaments and other goods, crude exchanged in one part of the world for crude sold at a discounted price in another. The spot price for crude in Amsterdam has usually been below the official OPEC price.

OPEC has demonstrated both the power and the weaknesses of cartels. The profits gained by the early restriction on production have no parallels in cartel history; but they also led to the organisation being undermined from within and without.

Competition will out. A final means of accommodating oligopolistic interdependence is for competitors to allow for the existence of one another by observing prudent rules of thumb.

6 COST-PLUS PRICING

Price theory attempts to explain price determination, not to describe it. Objections on the lines that 'manufacturers do not equate marginal cost with marginal revenue, they do not even know what marginal cost and marginal revenue are: what they do is take average variable cost, add on a margin to cover overheads and profit, and so arrive at the price' are therefore mostly beside the point. There are two situations, however, where cost-plus pricing may have explanatory as well as descriptive power: first, where potential entry is a threat and costs are used to estimate the level of entry price, and secondly, where there is monopoly or oligopolists co-ordinate their prices to maximise profits jointly. In the second case cost-plus pricing is an alternative formulation of profit maximisation to marginalism.

Potential competition

When there are only a small number of suppliers, but entry into a trade is easy, the existing suppliers need to take potential rivals into account. They need to estimate the price at which new rivals may be attracted, and a ready method of making such estimates is on the basis of their own costs. When they do this, demand and cost categories intermingle. A manufacturer judges that if his price exceeds the entry level he will lose sales very rapidly, and the price level at which this elastic demand is met is estimated from costs.

The mechanics of price determination are illustrated in Figure 7.5,

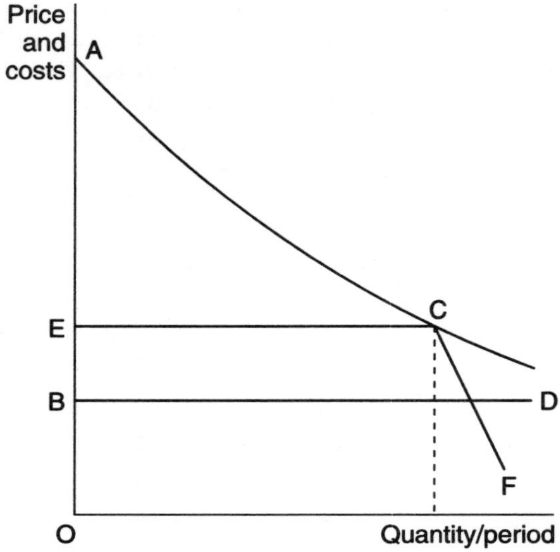

Figure 7.5 Cost-plus pricing with potential competition

where AC represents average total cost, BD constant average variable costs, and ECF demand from the point of view of a firm. Price is OE or OB plus a mark-up of BE. When average variable cost is not constant, it is usual to take average variable cost at some conventional level of output, say 80 per cent of capacity.

This model does not contradict arguments in terms of marginal cost and marginal revenue because marginal revenue is undefined at the level of output chosen where the individual demand curve has a pronounced kink. It does, however, place proper emphasis on the need to take account of competition from all sides and of the factors affecting the level of entry price. Cost-plus theories easily accommodate the variety of considerations, including those of finance and liquidity, that may enter into the determination of the gross profit margin. They also provide a convenient formulation of the reaction of pricing in individual firms during periods of inflation.[13]

Cost-plus pricing and monopoly

The second cost-plus pricing model is not an alternative to

mainstream theory, but a possible formulation of the theory of monopoly pricing when average variable cost is constant. It applies equally to a group of oligopolists intent on joint profit maximisation. It was shown in note 1 of Chapter 6 that when elasticity of demand is measured as an absolute quantity:

$$\text{price} = \text{marginal revenue} \times \frac{\text{elasticity of demand}}{\text{elasticity of demand} - 1}$$

When profit is maximised, marginal cost equals marginal revenue, and therefore at the most profitable output:

$$\text{price} = \text{marginal cost} \times \frac{\text{elasticity of demand}}{\text{elasticity of demand} - 1}$$

If average variable cost is constant, marginal cost equals average variable cost, and at the most profitable output:

$$\text{price} = \text{average variable cost} \times \frac{\text{elasticity of demand}}{\text{elasticity of demand} - 1}$$

This may be expressed in cost-plus terms. For example, if the elasticity of demand is 3, price equals average variable cost multiplied by 3/2 or average variable cost plus 50 per cent.

7 SUMMARY

- The main characteristic of oligopoly is the direct dependence of one supplier's fortunes not only on his own decisions but also on those of a small number of rivals. All members of the economy are ultimately linked by the market system: in oligopoly the participants can feel the linkages.
- Early theories of Cournot, Bertrand, Edgeworth and Sweezy continue to have influence because they point to possible outcomes: price between monopoly and competitive levels, competitive prices, fluctuating prices and rigid prices.
- They also incorporate the distinctive equilibrium of oligopoly, the Nash equilibrium, where each participant does the best he can in the knowledge that each of his rivals is doing the best he can. Nash equilibrium is a feature of game theory.
- Game theory provides a formal means of analysing interdependent decision-making with starting conditions, permissible strategies and available payoffs fully specified. The prisoners' dilemma

game is widely applied because its structure forces the outcome. It exposes possible wastes of competition; but it is less portentous when played over successive periods.

- Suppliers can always improve their joint profit by avoiding competition, and in oligopoly this possibility may influence market behaviour. Oligopolists may compete in price until no more than normal profits are earned, or they may collude to gain monopoly profits.
- Joint profit maximisation may be achieved by suppliers accepting one of their number as a monopolistic price leader; but a price leader may simply be the strongest competitor whose low costs act as a restraint on the prices of rivals, or the dominant firm content to take the supplies of a competitive fringe for granted whilst choosing its price. A final possibility is that a price leader may be no more than a business barometer registering the equilibrium response to changes in cost or demand.
- Cartel agreements are vulnerable to outside competition and to internal strains as members compete in quality, advertising or surreptitious price-cuts.
- Cartels may act as cohesive monopolies which may be analysed as if they were single firms, or competitive manoeuvring may shift from the market-place to the conference table. In the latter case oligopoly theory must be incorporated into explanations of cartel prices.
- When barriers to entry are low, prices may be explained on a cost-plus basis, the margin above average variable cost depending upon the full cost of potential entrants.
- Cost-plus pricing may also be a formulation of profit maximisation by a monopolist or by oligopolists co-ordinating their prices: in these cases the margin depends upon the elasticity of demand.
- Oligopoly theory points to pragmatism. At one time some economists argued that market structure determined market behaviour and market behaviour determined market performance. Oligopolistic market structures are compatible with all sorts of behaviour. It is not possible to jump from market structure to dogmatic judgement of performance.

8

MARKET PROBLEMS: INFORMATION, EXTERNALITIES AND PROPERTY RIGHTS

1 INTRODUCTION

Markets are fascinating. The 'result of human action, but not of human design', they perform very creditably when compared with deliberately designed institutions. However, they are not without defects. In Chapter 6 it was seen that monopolised markets may be characterised by outputs that are undesirably low, prices that are undesirably high, dead-weight loss, and questionable income transfers. Problems of monopoly carry over into oligopolistic markets, and oligopolists may find themselves in prisoners' dilemmas with increased expenditures that cancel out without achieving any purpose.

This chapter adds further reservations. Three general problems are examined, the adequacy of information, the completeness of cost calculations, and the effectiveness of property laws. The next section discusses the perverse effects of inadequate information in markets for 'lemons', the need for consumer protection in markets for 'faith goods', and wastes of advertising. Section 3 is devoted to the economic basis of environmentalist worries. Costs of despoiling the environment may fail to register in private accounts guiding market decisions. Section 4 examines problems of fishing when there is open access to fishing grounds.

These topics are often discussed by welfare economists under the heading 'market failure'. This terminology is fair in the sense that they are hardly market successes; but it may be misleading in that other arrangements, such as state control, may be no better and the problem of open access to natural resources is one of absent rather than badly working markets.

2 THE ECONOMICS OF IGNORANCE

Sellers typically know more about the goods they offer than do buyers, a situation suggested by the Latin tag *caveat emptor*, let the buyer beware. Yet this unequal knowledge does not usually give rise to problems. Consumers are protected by the efforts of all but fly-by-night traders to build up goodwill. Brands gain value by certifying consistent quality, and the level of quality is often underwritten by heavy investment in advertising. These protections work well for experience goods, such as breakfast cereals and soaps, which are known before repeat purchase, and for search goods, such as computers and new cars, that are bought after extensive shopping around, study of consumer tests and chats with friends and neighbours. Problems arise with two remaining groups of goods, 'lemons' and 'faith goods'.

Markets for lemons

'Buying a lemon' is Wodehouse for 'buying a pup', the unlucky purchase of a defective item. It has been associated with a particular market situation by G.A. Akerlof.[1] A market for lemons is one where there is unequal information about qualities and characteristics of goods on the part of sellers and buyers, and in addition uncertainty about these qualities and characteristics. An example is provided by the market in second-hand cars. Used cars of a given vintage vary from very good to very bad, and it is difficult for a buyer to identify the lemons before purchase. In these circumstances a buyer is not prepared to pay more than the value of a car of average quality. If one has a good car to sell, however, the price of an average car would be a bad deal, and the best cars will be held off the market. The average quality of used cars on the market will therefore fall, the price offered will fall, cars of better quality than the new average will be withheld, and the average quality will fall further. This process could go on until the only second-hand cars for sale would be lemons.

The lemon danger helps to explain the sudden fall in price that occurs when a new car is driven out of the showroom. The resale price is likely to be 20 per cent lower than the new price. When a car is bought in the showroom there is no certainty that the new car will perform exactly according to specification: it may be a dream car or a 'Monday-morning job' with every tolerance at the minimum level. The probability distribution of quality for new cars varies between makes and is taken into account in the price a motorist is prepared to pay. If the new owner should wish to resell quickly, his car will be suspect and regarded as belonging to a new, less attractive, probability distribution of quality.

Markets for lemons are sweetened by the intervention of reputable dealers, the services of professional surveyors, provision of guarantees and opportunities to purchase on approval. It is evident, however, that unequal information available to parties on each side of the market, and uncertainty about the quality of items traded, gives rise to problems. There are too many hidden hands at work in such trades.

Faith goods

The position would be worse if welfare were left to the working of free market forces in exchanges of faith goods. As the name implies, these goods are bought on faith. It is possible that a consumer does not know what he wants before he makes a purchase, and does not know what he has received in return for payment.

The most important examples relate to health. It is to be hoped that health treatment is not so frequent that it becomes an experience good, and there is usually not time for it to become a search good. When a patient consults a doctor he does so because he does not know what is wrong with him, and, even if he subsequently recovers in health, he cannot be sure that this would not have happened in any case, possibly despite the efforts of the doctor. Similarly, medicines may be appropriate or inappropriate, harmless, effective or harmful. If markets in such faith goods were left unregulated they would provide golden opportunities for charlatans and conmen. The solution is to have official certification of doctors and government testing of the safety of drugs.

The problem of purchasing faith goods occurs in less-dangerous fields wherever repairs are needed to equipment. If a car breaks down, the average motorist does not know what he needs nor what he has paid for when his car is repaired. Car manufacturers intervene to license garages as their agents, and trade associations seek to check the behaviour of members so that all may gain reputation and goodwill. Faith goods have in the past provided dubious opportunities for advertising, especially in patent medicines.

Advertising

About 1.5 per cent of the gross national product, or 2.2 per cent of consumers' total expenditure, is devoted to advertising. Absorbing so many resources one might expect advertising to be very intrusive rather than simply intrusive; but a lot is classified, trade or retailers' advertising that passes by those not interested. The advertising that cannot easily be escaped, manufacturer–consumer advertising, makes up about two-fifths of the total: it is specially noticeable because so much of it is concentrated on patent medicines, cosmetics, toiletries, detergents, drink, tobacco and confectionery.

A distinction is often made between informative and persuasive advertising; but it is not always easy to separate the two. A bare proclamation 'Try Me' carries information about availability as well as some persuasion, and the slogan 'Never Knowingly Undersold' carries persuasion as well as some information.

Informative advertising

The obvious service of advertising is in drawing attention to new products; but it may also help with established commodities. Acquiring information about market opportunities is costly to consumers. It takes time which could be devoted to paid employment, housework or leisure. Shopping around is sometimes pleasurable but often exhausting. Hence it is seldom if ever worth while to become fully informed. The optimum rule is the usual one: seek information up to the point where the marginal benefit from additional knowledge equals the marginal cost of acquisition.

The process of becoming optimally informed may be seen in a simple model where there is dispersion of prices about a ruling level. The gain from search is the reduction in price that need be paid. Suppose that prices of some good are evenly distributed between £20 and £25, and search is random. The expected price from a first reconnaissance is £22.50. There is a 50:50 chance that this could be improved on. The expected reduction attainable by a second search is one-half of £2.50, an expected value of £1.25. There is a 25:75 chance that one more search will turn up a lower price: the expected reduction from a third search is one-half of £1.25, an expected value of 62.5p. As the number of prices discovered increases, the chance of bettering those already known falls and the probable size of any improvement also falls. A point will be reached where the probable gain from further information is no greater than the additional cost of acquisition. Just how comprehensive the search will be depends upon the ease of acquiring price information. Advertising may ease matters either directly by informing about prices or indirectly by drawing attention to alternative suppliers.

If consumers become better informed the dispersion of prices should be reduced as suppliers asking high prices lose custom. This proposition has been tested in the United States where some states impose restrictions on advertising and some do not. The best-known study is that of Lee Benham who found that prices of eyeglasses were lower in states that allowed opticians to advertise.[2] Benham's influence spanned the Atlantic when the British government removed restrictions on advertising by opticians. Similar results have been found with prescription drugs in the USA. The dispersion of prices for gasoline has also been found to be greater in states that restrict price advertising.[3]

The Consumers' Association is not prejudiced in favour of advertised products, yet, in their first 1,000 investigations, 70 per cent of recommended best buys were for heavily advertised goods.[4] It must be conceded that advertising performs a service of information; but it still leaves a feeling that one is being got at.

Persuasive advertising – the dependence effect

J.K. Galbraith has argued with typical panache that wants are created by the firms that satisfy them:

> The . . . direct link between production and wants is provided by the institutions of modern advertising and salesmanship. These cannot be reconciled with the notion of independently determined desires, for their central function is to create desires – to bring into being wants that previously did not exist. This is accomplished by the producer of the goods at his behest. A broad empirical relationship exists between what is spent on production of consumers' goods and what is spent in synthesising the desire for that production . . . Outlays for the manufacturing of a product are not more important in the strategy of modern business

> enterprise than outlays for manufacturing of demand for the product.

Pointing the moral, he argues:

> Consumer wants can have bizarre, frivolous, or even immoral origins, and an admirable case can still be made for a society that seeks to satisfy them. But the case cannot stand if it is the process of satisfying wants that creates the wants. For then the individual who urges the importance of production to satisfy these wants is precisely in the position of the onlooker who applauds the efforts of the squirrel to keep abreast of the wheel that is propelled by his own efforts.[5]

It is not difficult to find instances of consumption responding to advertising. For example, in the late 1970s John Smith's bitter lost market share in Yorkshire to its rivals Tetley, Trophy and Stones. Young drinkers (18–24) in particular saw the hand-pumped, cask-conditioned Tetley bitter as the drink for knowledgeable drinkers. Between 1980 and 1982 their attitudes were turned around. John Smith's bitter was unchanged, price remained in line with the competition, and pub standards did not change. The difference was made by a big increase in television advertising of 'Big John' which persuaded young drinkers that John Smith was the macho drink.[6]

Alcohol and nicotine are the two addictive drugs causing most drug-related illnesses and deaths in Britain, and the part played by advertising in promoting their use is a cause for concern. However, advertising is only one among the social and group pressures driving people to drink and smoke. The process of persuasion is more uncertain than Galbraith makes out.

First, the wrong people may get the message. For many years, Guinness, with a zoo full of animals making off with the keeper's stout (My Goodness! My Guinness!) had great success in appealing to twelve-year-old schoolgirls whilst its customers were mainly male and over thirty-five. If the right people get the message they may not understand it. Smirnoff used advertisements showing a wall with odd scrawls of graffiti such as 'I thought the Kama Sutra was an Indian restaurant until I discovered Smirnoff': market researchers surveying potential customers found that 60 per cent of them thought that the Kama Sutra was indeed an Indian restaurant. If the right people get the message and understand it, they may forget it: tests show very small recall of advertising messages. Finally, if the right people get the message, understand it and remember it, they may not act upon it. In the end, the assertion of the dependence effect is an assertion that advertising elasticities of demand are large.

Advertising elasticity

The advertising elasticity of demand usually refers to the demand enjoyed by an individual firm and is measured by the ratio of the percentage change in quantity demanded to the percentage change in advertising expenditure, other things (notably price and quality of product) being equal.

There are some reasons for expecting advertising elasticities to decline as advertising expenditure increases: good prospects are likely to be reached first, and there is a progressive diminution in the number of unreached potential customers. Market communication is in some respects like the spread of contagious disease: 1 infects 2 who infect 4 who infect 8 and so on, but after a time the 128th, say, who attempts to infect two more fails because they have already been infected and the process begins to peter out. In the area of advertising where effectiveness may be immediately measured, mail order, it is found that increasing the number of insertions of an advertisement does not increase replies proportionately.

Advertising elasticity may therefore vary with the level of advertising just as price elasticity varies with the level of price. In any case advertising elasticities are seldom large. For example, S.F. Witt and C.L. Pass, examining the effects of health warnings and advertising on the demand for cigarettes, estimate the advertising elasticity to be about 0.07, that is, a 1 per cent increase in advertising expenditure leads to a 0.07 per cent increase in quantity demanded.[7] K. Cowling estimated advertising elasticities for cars of 0.19, tractors 0.49, margarine 0.59, coffee 0.14, and toothpaste 0.24.[8]

It can be shown that a profit-maximising firm setting its advertising budget independently of rivals will vary expenditure directly with the advertising elasticity of demand and inversely with the price elasticity. The direct relationship is straightforward: the more responsive sales are to advertising the greater the advertising. The inverse relationship with price elasticity arises because a price cut is an alternative to an increase in advertising expenditure. A price cut costs lost revenue on the existing level of sales, but provides revenue on additional sales at the lower price. The greater the elasticity of demand, the greater the gain in revenue on new sales and the smaller the loss of revenue on the starting level of sales: price reductions are therefore more attractive than increases in advertising the greater is the price elasticity of demand. This is the reasoning behind the Dorfman–Steiner theorem that, with constant product quality and constant advertising expenditure by rivals, a firm will maximise profits when:

$$\frac{\text{advertising outlay}}{\text{sales revenue}} = \frac{\text{advertising elasticity of demand}}{\text{price elasticity of demand}}$$

The theorem is restricted to independent decisions, and does not apply in oligopoly markets where rivals force one another into mutually offsetting expenditures.[9]

Elasticities are reminders that many assertions about advertising are measurable and some of the most heated controversies capable of reduction to matters of fact. In similar way, measurement may contract controversy about pollution.

3 MARKETS AND THE ENVIRONMENT

Two sets of economic concepts are available for analysing environmental problems: externalities and optimalities. We seek to identify external costs and benefits associated with spoiling or enhancing the environment, and to identify the economic objective of 'optimum pollution' or 'optimum purification'. This may seem excessively dispassionate where heavy metals, persistent chemicals, nuclear wastes, global warming, ozone depletion, and irreversible processes are concerned; but the analysis does not assert that the optimum may never be very small, simply that one needs to measure costs and benefits before reaching any conclusion.

External costs and benefits

External costs are borne by people outside the boundaries of responsibility of decision-makers in the market. For example, £5 million has been spent repairing the fabric of Westminster Abbey damaged by atmospheric pollution; but this cost played no part in the decisions of industrialists and motorists discharging sulphur dioxide and nitrogen oxides into the air. On the brighter side, external benefits accrue to outsiders. For example, the air has been cleared of a good deal of dirt by the substitution of gas and oil for coal in heating and transportation: London pea-souper fogs are things of the past, and soot no longer falls like snowflakes in Sheffield.[10]

These spillover, or neighbourhood, effects occur in production and consumption, for example:

	External costs	*External benefits*
In production	pollution land dereliction over-fishing	drainage staff training marketing techniques
In consumption	traffic congestion graffiti portable radios	education art patronage house improvements

The trouble with externalities is that by their very nature they escape the cash nexus of market transactions.[11] The market may therefore provide an excessive quantity of a good because account is not taken of the full cost, or an insufficient quantity because account is not taken of the full benefit. In diagrammatic terms, the market supply curve, depicting private marginal costs, needs to have external costs added vertically if it is to represent the full social cost of production. This modified supply curve will cut the market demand curve to the left of the private equilibrium point. In Figure 8.1(a), a freely working market would provide OA per period, a level at which marginal social cost (private cost plus external cost) exceeds demand price (private marginal benefit) by BC: marginal social cost exceeds marginal benefit until output is contracted to OD.

Where external benefits are involved the market would supply too little. The demand curve depicting marginal satisfaction of paying customers needs to have the value of external benefits added vertically to indicate the full social benefit of supply. Figure 8.1(b) illustrates such a case. The social optimum would be OE, but the market would only supply OF.

There are five remedies available for dealing with external costs:

1. the government might regulate production and prescribe an output of OD;
2. the victims suffering the external costs could be compensated by BC per unit of output;

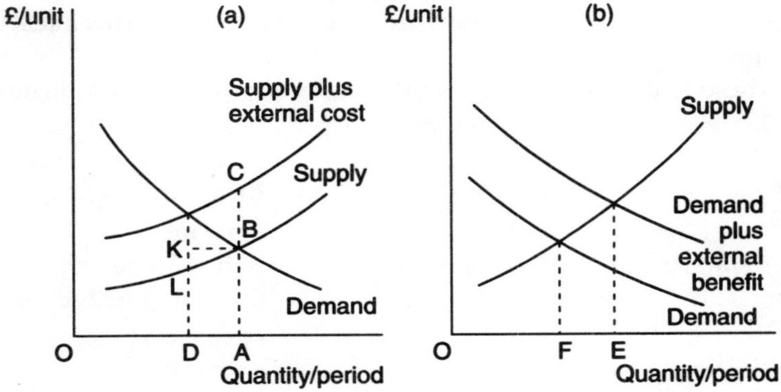

Figure 8.1 External costs and benefits

3. suppliers could be bribed to restrict production by a payment exceeding their loss of producers' surplus, that is, an amount exceeding KLB;
4. suppliers could be taxed BC per unit supplied, that is, a tax equalling the external cost;
5. outsiders suffering external costs could become members of supplying firms so that external costs would be internalised.

There are five corresponding policies where external benefits are involved that could lead suppliers, depicted in Figure 8.1(b), to provide OE per period instead of OF. These same remedies will be met again when considering policies for dealing with pollution.

Optimum pollution

Avoidance of pollution, like other social objectives, is not an absolute. 'Absolute virtue is as sure to kill a man as absolute vice is', and if purity were sought before aught else we should all starve very hygienically. The gains from cleanliness must be weighed against the costs of attaining it. The appropriate economic objective is optimum pollution, or, if preferred, optimum cleanliness, where the marginal benefit from enhancing the environment just equals the marginal cost of enhancement. If marginal benefit exceeded marginal cost further cleansing would be in order.

The costs of reducing pollution consist of the labour and equipment devoted to abatement plus the value of any output forgone from reducing levels of activity contributing to pollution. For example, the costs of reducing air pollution from car exhausts consists of costs of fitting cleaner engines and catalytic converters, and possibly the value of journeys given up. Figure 8.2 illustrates the marginal costs and benefits, and net benefits or net costs, of reducing pollution. The level of pollution is measured horizontally from O, filth, to P, purity. The marginal cost of pollution abatement is shown by OA, the marginal cost of level of cleanliness R being RS and the total cost of cleansing to this level area ORS.

Marginal benefits are depicted by BP: the marginal benefit of level of cleanliness R being once more RS and the total benefit from attaining this level area OBSR. The net benefit of this situation is shown by the vertical hatched area OBS. Benefits may consist of improved health, greater comfort, reduced costs of old activities and possibilities of new activities. For instance, in the case of river pollution benefits may accrue from reduced costs of treatment when water is drawn off for industrial or domestic use, and also from new resorts for fish and fishing.

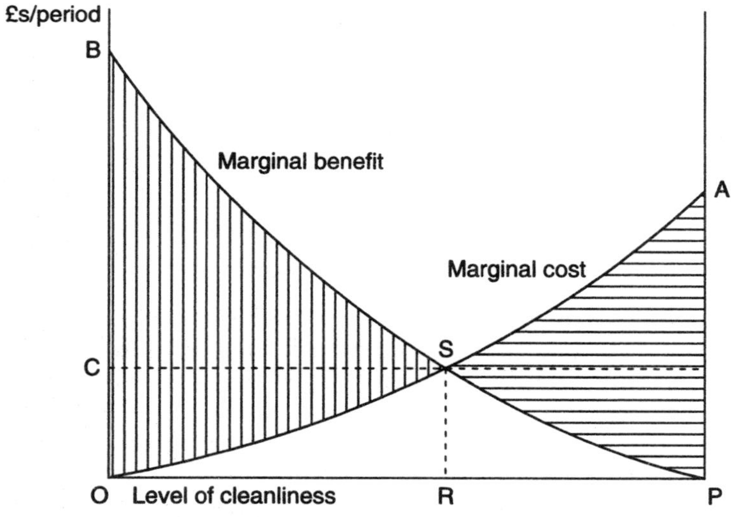

Figure 8.2 Optimum pollution

The optimum level of pollution in Figure 8.2 is evidently R, where net benefit is maximised. At R some pollution damage remains, depicted by area RSP; but increasing cleansing beyond R would involve greater costs than benefits, the net loss of the horizontally hatched area SAP.

Cost-benefit estimates

Estimating costs and benefits of pollution abatement poses problems. The direct costs of abatement are usually available but indirect costs may be more difficult to identify and quantify. There are further difficulties in placing values on improvements to the environment. Improvements come in many forms. For example, sulphur dioxide emissions from power stations reduce agricultural yields, damage timber, pollute water supplies, corrode property and damage health. Cleansing discharges would yield improvements in all these areas. Each area expands with the vision of the analyst. The effect on agriculture may simply be a reduction in harvests, or it may include costs of changed farming methods, damage to landscape and wildlife habitats, losses to ramblers, the tourist trade and so on. There is also the question of whether attention should be restricted to one neighbourhood or should take into account export of pollution downstream or downwind and across political boundaries. Such practical problems may easily be multiplied; but it must be borne in mind that there is no point in worrying over things we do not know or things that could not be found out for less cost than the information would be worth. Practical problems of cost-benefit analysis do not prevent better policies being adopted to deal with pollution.

Pollution policies: regulation

The obvious way for dealing with pollution is to forbid it. If the optimum level of pollution is R, polluters may be prescribed effluents that are consistent with R. However, administrators have to determine these prescriptions. Permission to pollute equally would favour those not doing much pollution and ignore costs of reducing pollution. Permits requiring proportionate reductions in pollution also ignore costs. It is not efficient to require some polluters to incur high costs of purification when the same reduction in pollution could be attained by others at less cost.

Differing costs of pollution control may be accommodated by allowing trade in pollution permits. Those with low costs are given an incentive to reduce pollution and sell their rights to those engaged in dirtier activities. There have been experiments with such permits, 'emission reduction credits', in the United States but markets in permits have been slow to develop. British power generators are allowed to distribute their total emission permit between their own stations, but not to trade permits with one another.

The basic trouble with regulations, however, is that they have to be enforced and the costs of compliance provide an inbuilt incentive for avoidance or evasion. British firms have for many years had levels of effluent prescribed, yet when Trent Water Authority took over in 1974 it reported twelve organisations exceeding consent conditions, including the British Sugar Corporation, the Milk Marketing Board, the British Steel Corporation and the National Coal Board (all at the time statutory bodies). Forty companies refused permission for the Authority to disclose fully details of one effluent or more – companies including such giants as British Petroleum, Dunlop and ICI. The costs of enforcing regulations have to be kept in mind as well as the difficulties of framing regulations.

Compensating pollutees

A second possibility is to provide compensation for victims of pollution. The damage suffered from pollution consists of benefit forgone, shown in Figure 8.2 by areas below the marginal benefit curve. If polluters were required to compensate those suffering, it would pay them to reduce pollution so long as the cost of abatement was less than benefit endangered, that is, up to the point of optimum pollution. In Figure 8.2 marginal costs of abatement begin to exceed marginal benefits beyond R, and compensation equal to RSP would be less onerous than costs RSAP.

Recompensing polluters

The roles of villain and victim may be reversed by historical circumstances. A polluter may have been first on the scene and have established a historical right to discharge effluent. Latecomers suffering from these activities could offer recompense for limiting pollution. Somewhat surprisingly, the recompense would lead once more to the optimum level of pollution. A polluter would maintain purity level R, in Figure 8.2, so long as recompense exceeded area ORS and sufferers would be able to recompense up to the area OBSR. It would not be worth while for sufferers to offer recompense for purity beyond R because the cost of abatement would exceed the benefit to be gained.

R.H. Coase pointed out that compensation of pollutees or recompense of polluters could be left to private negotiation between the parties so long as property rights to be free from pollution or to be free to pollute were fully defined.[12] Furthermore, in the absence of costs of negotiation, the same optimum level of pollution would be reached irrespective of who possessed the property rights. The distribution of income would differ with the disposition of rights but, as seen in the calculations of compensation or recompense, the scope for negotiation is the same.

Leaving pollution problems to be sorted out by the parties involved has some attractions, especially for lawyers. It is not a practical proposition, however, when there are large numbers of parties. Definition of property rights in pollution faces the same difficulties as the definition of costs and benefits in cost–benefit analysis. Private property rights have provided some protection from pollution under English Common Law. For example, the Central Electricity Generating Board was ordered by the courts to stop discharging warm water into the Trent because this killed fish and infringed local fishing rights.

Pollution charges

A further policy option is to charge polluters for the right to pollute. So long as the marginal cost of abatement is less than the charge a potential polluter will curtail his discharges, and if the fee is fixed at the level at which marginal cost of abatement equals the marginal benefit optimum pollution is once more achieved. In Figure 8.2, a charge of OC per unit of pollution would do the trick, and yield some revenue to the controllers. Pollution charges share the administrative problems of regulation in determining the target level of pollution, but provide a financial incentive for enforcement. Sums raised might cover, or more than cover, costs of enforcement although the logic of the proposal is not to make polluters pay for the costs of controlling their activities.

Internalise externalities

Finally, as the problem is caused by the existence of external costs, it may be possible to eliminate the pollution problems by bringing everyone concerned within the same boundaries. For example, sewage is discharged into rivers raw or, in developed countries, after various levels of treatment. The pollution caused varies with expenditure on treatment. Water is drawn from rivers for domestic purposes, and the cost of water supply depends upon the amount of purification necessary. Economic efficiency requires that treatment should be given to effluent or off-take depending on relative cost. This has been arranged in Britain since 1974 by making the same authority responsible for sewerage and water supply.

The five policies described are not mutually exclusive. In 1969, millions of dead fish came floating down the Rhine because of an accidental discharge of insecticide from a French chemical works. Rotterdam was forced to depend on emergency water supplies for three days. This was an alarming catastrophe, but to anyone familiar with the Mersey it was also a surprise. How could there be so many fish in the Rhine? After all, this river carries a greater volume of effluent than its natural flow, and passes very heavily industrialised areas. Part of the answer lies with the co-operative of local authorities, industrial firms, sewerage and water supply undertakings that sells fresh water and disposes of liquid waste in the Rhur. The co-operative internalises external costs and benefits. It fixes charges for industrial effluent from members equal to the cost of diluting effluent to the level of purity at which fish can live. The fish population had recovered in time to be poisoned by another accidental discharge of chemicals, from a Swiss firm, in 1987.

Pollution is a problem; but it is a problem with many solutions. Fish have to contend with fishermen as well as polluters.

4 MARKETS AND PROPERTY RIGHTS

Fishing grounds have traditionally been regarded as common property where all are free to compete for use with no exclusive or transferable rights. Markets do not work well in these circumstances. A stock of fish is a valuable natural resource capable of yielding an income to the community from year to year; but when no one has an exclusive right to this income it may be absorbed in the cost of inputs dedicated to its winning.

Competition between fishermen may be carried to the point where they earn no more than the alternative earnings of their labour and capital in other activities. The nature of this 'dissipation of rent' may be seen in a highly stylised model of a fishery.

Assume that there is pure competition in the markets for fish and for inputs into fishing. This is fairly realistic. Assume that there is only one kind of fish which swims in a clearly defined fishing area. This might apply to crabs or lobsters; but is obviously a drastic simplification. Assume that there is a standard unit of fishing effort: a standard boat with standard gear manned by crews of given size and efficiency. Assume that everyone has open access to the fishing ground. This would have applied until exclusive economic interests were asserted for areas stretching two hundred miles from coastal states, and government regulations became common. Finally, assume that the biology of the fish also conforms to a simple model.

Figure 8.3 shows the evolution of the fishery. The total catch is measured vertically, the catch being measured in units of £1-worth of fish so that the same scale indicates both the quantity and value of the fish. Fishing effort is measured to the right from O and the fish stock to the left from S. Catch, stock and effort are interrelated. At O, before fishing begins the stock of fish is at its natural level, recruitment into the population and growth in fish size just balancing

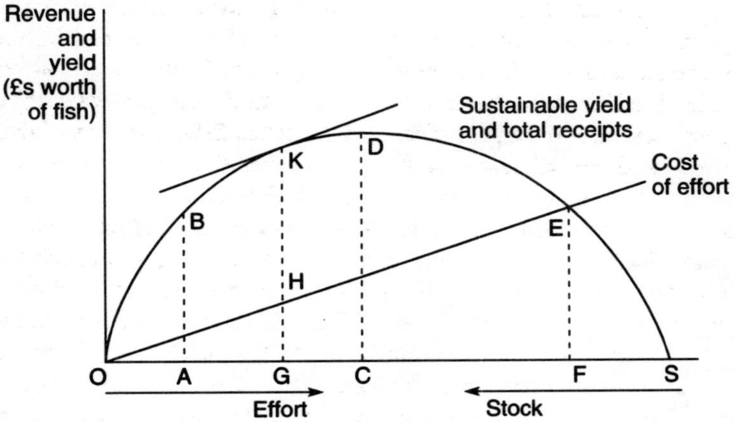

Figure 8.3 Fishing levels

losses from age, disease and natural predation. Fishing effort reduces the size of the stock but at the same time improves the prospects of recruits and leaves more food for survivors. A small fishing effort, associated with a large stock would make possible a sustainable yield, from season to season, such as AB. The curve OS plots sustainable yields. At first the sustainable yield rises because reductions in the size of the stock increases the ecological space for fish to grow; but a point must be reached of maximum sustainable yield. Beyond this point the surviving stock is not large enough to provide replacements, and as the stock falls the sustainable yield falls. At S the fish have been fished out.

It is not clear what size of stock and sustainable yield the fish would prefer. At O they are as nature intended; but at D they have an easier life until caught. They would clearly not choose points on the sustainable yield curve beyond D where fewer fish enjoy shorter lives: nor would anyone concerned with economic efficiency. Sustainable catches equalling those to the right of D could be obtained with less effort to the left of D. Biologists often favour the maximum sustainable yield as the optimum operation of a fishery; but this is in excess of the economic optimum. At D the rate of change of total receipts is zero, that is, marginal receipts are zero, and this could only be an economic optimum if fishing effort were costless. Fish, biologists and economists all deplore fishing effort greater than OC, but a freely working competitive market may easily produce such an outcome.

OE depicts the total cost of fishing effort, including normal profit, rising at a constant rate because of the assumption of a standard unit of fishing effort: average cost of effort and marginal cost of effort are constant. So long as total receipts exceed total costs abnormally high profits are earned as fishermen lay claim to the rent of the fishery, and there is an incentive to increase fishing effort. This incentive remains until total receipts equal total costs and the rent of the fishery has been dissipated in enhanced fishing costs. This free market equilibrium is to the right of D. In more realistic circumstances it might be a very fragile equilibrium. The sustainable yield curve shows a determinate relationship between effort, fish stock and sustainable yield. It would be in the interests of fishermen to conserve the stock SF because it would cost more to go beyond E than the fish are worth. In reality this stock might be insufficient to withstand a chance shock to the fishing environment.

The economic optimum fishing effort would be determined by the return to extra effort and the cost of extra effort. In Figure 8.3 the optimum effort is OG, where marginal cost equals marginal receipts from the fishery, and a sustainable rent of HK accrues to society. There are a large variety of policies that could achieve this optimum. Effort could be limited to OG by licensing of boats, thus enabling the permitted boats to enjoy the economic rent, or, if licences were transferable, enabling the licensees to enjoy the capital value of the permits. Harvests could be taxed by the amount of the economic rent so that normal profit would be the most obtainable at the optimum catch, or effort could be taxed so that the total costs are brought into equality with total receipts at the optimum catch. The trouble with all such policies is that they aim to reduce the use of scarce resources in fishing; but they all have the short-run impact of destroying fishermen's livelihoods. When governments seek to conserve fish stocks they are likely to be attracted to policies that increase fishing costs by reducing fishing efficiency, for example, by limiting the size of boats, the mesh of nets or total allowable catches.

5 SUMMARY

- Markets work badly when participants are ill-informed, outsiders are affected by market transactions, and property rights are not fully defined.
- When buyers and sellers have unequal and uncertain information about the quality and characteristics of goods traded, a market may degenerate into one dealing only with low-quality items, that is, lemons.
- Faith goods present opportunities for dishonest trading in the absence of outside certifying and testing authorities.
- Advertising may reduce search costs of consumers, enabling them to find lower-cost supplies: the dispersion of prices is narrowed.
- The power of advertising may easily be exaggerated if possibilities of advertising being misdirected, misunderstood, forgotten or ignored are not taken into account: this is attested by low advertising elasticities of demand.
- A profit-maximising firm that decides its advertising budget independently will spend more on advertising the greater the advertising elasticity of demand and the lower the price elasticity of demand.

- External costs and benefits are ignored by freely working markets, and in consequence supplies of goods involving external costs are too large and those of goods involving external benefits are too small.
- Pollution is an important example of external costs. Optimum pollution is the efficient economic objective attained when the marginal benefit of reduced pollution equals the marginal cost of such amelioration.
- Five kinds of policy may be adopted to attain optimum pollution: regulation, compensation of pollutees, recompense of polluters, charging for the right to pollute, and internalising externalities.
- Compensation or recompense could be negotiated across markets if it should prove possible to define property rights in freedom from pollution or freedom to pollute.
- Common property rights, that is, rights that exclude no one from use of resources, invite competition to the point where each user earns no more than he could elsewhere and the value of the common property is dissipated in excess capacity.

Part IV

FACTOR MARKETS

9

MARGINAL PRODUCTIVITY AND FACTOR DEMAND

1 INTRODUCTION

The marginal productivity theory of distribution establishes two propositions. First, the quantity of a factor's services demanded per period varies inversely with its price because of technological constraints on productivity and marketing constraints on the sale of additional output. Secondly, in competitive markets, when firms maximise profits, the wage or price paid for a factor measures the value of its marginal product. Sections 2 and 3 are devoted to the first proposition, and section 4 applies the second to brain drains and international capital movements.

2 ASPECTS OF TECHNOLOGY

Production takes millions of different forms. It goes on down mines, across fields, inside workshops, factories, breweries and distilleries, in warehouses, supermarkets and corner shops, along roads, railways, sea and air routes. All sorts of crafts and technologies are involved, the mining engineer's knowledge of ventilation, the farmer's skill in animal husbandry, the furnace-minder's knowledge of metals, the engineer's knowledge of stresses, the weaver's feel for cloth, the designer's flair for fashion, the buyer's awareness of alternative supplies, the retailer's empathy with his customers, expertise in programming, in circuitry and so on. Yet if we strip away the special features of the individual case, all may be seen as examples of the transformation of inputs into outputs.

Viewing production in this abstract way it is possible to isolate relationships between input and input, and between inputs and outputs, and to identify the conditions determining these relationships. Three merit special attention:

1. opportunities for substituting one input for another whilst maintaining the rate of output constant;
2. the response of output when inputs are increased in constant proportion, which may be proportionate, more than proportionate or less than proportionate, depending upon returns to scale;
3. the response of output when one input is varied and other inputs are held constant.

These three relationships may be seen in stylised form if it is assumed that only two divisible inputs are involved. Divisibility allows quantities of inputs to be varied continuously. The sources of factor services are often divisible as a physical fact: raw materials may be used in grams, kilograms or tonnes. When the source of a service is indivisible, the service itself may be available in finely divided amounts: one cannot employ half a plumber, but there is no difficulty in hiring half a day's plumbing. Two divisible inputs is not many, but numbers may be augmented at will by considering relationships between pairs of inputs. In Figure 9.1, inputs X and Y are measured horizontally and output Z vertically. Points on the curved surface show the maximum output attainable with varying combinations of inputs.[1] This hill of output has been sliced in three ways: horizontally at constant heights, as along DG and HK; vertically along vectors from the origin, OC, OG and OK; and vertically parallel to the X and Y axes along AC and BC. The edges of horizontal slices are bowed towards the origin because declining amounts of one input require increasing amounts of the other to compensate. This follows logically from the fact that the inputs are different and hence not perfect substitutes for each other. Some technicalities may be seen in a specific example.

Substituting inputs

The hill of output may be depicted in contour lines by projecting curves such as HK on to the horizontal plane, providing an isoquant or equal-product map. Looking at road transport, Figure 9.2 shows the isoquant for 1 million truck-miles per year provided by alternative combinations of truck-hours and service-hours per year. At A, twenty trucks are used and 12,000 man-hours are

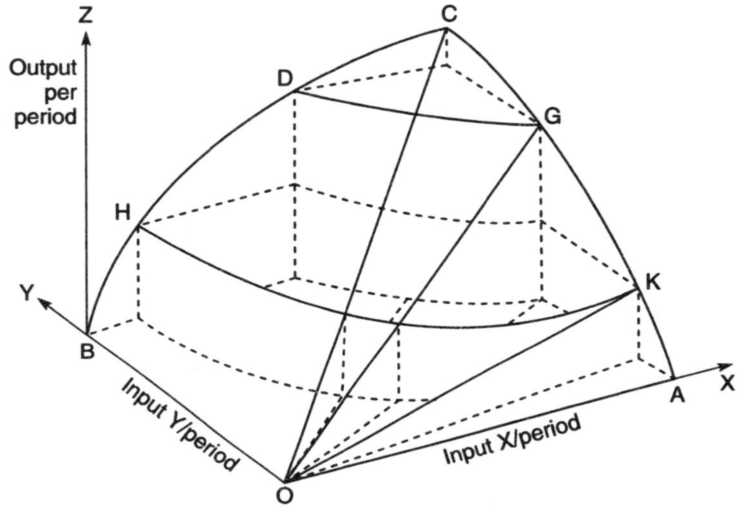

Figure 9.1 Production possibilities surface

devoted to servicing them: each truck would cover on average 50,000 miles per year and, if mechanics work 2,000 hours per year, six mechanics would be employed on maintenance. Fifty thousand miles is a low mileage for a commercial vehicle, and a little extra maintenance would enable a larger mileage to be achieved. At B, nineteen trucks are able to provide 1 million truck-miles per year, each truck travelling on average just over 52,600 miles. In order to operate at B maintenance work must be increased by 250 man-hours per year, so that between A and B 250 man-hours may be substituted for one truck. Between A and B, the rate of substitution of repair work for trucks is increment of repair work divided by decrement of trucks, or 250 man-hours per truck. As the number of trucks is reduced the mileage each must provide increases and so does the repair work needed to keep the trucks operating: between C and D 1,000 man-hours are needed to offset the loss of one truck, a rate of substitution of 1,000 man-hours per truck; and between E and F 4,000 additional man-hours are needed to offset the loss of one truck.

As man-hours of repair work are employed instead of trucks,

each successive reduction in the use of trucks necessitates a larger addition to repair work, in other words there is diminishing substitutability of repair work for trucks. The marginal productivity of mechanics falls as man-hours increase relative to truck hours, the marginal rate of substitution of mechanics for trucks equalling the ratio of the marginal productivity of trucks to that of mechanics. The implication for the demand for mechanics' services is that should wages fall relative to the rentals of trucks the quantity of servicing demanded would increase by an amount depending on the ease of substitution which varies with the extent of substitution.

Scale economies

Returning to Figure 9.1, the vertical slices along vector lines are shown as rising at a constant rate, indicating proportionate increases in output when all inputs are increased in a constant proportion, that is, constant returns to scale. Changes in output as the scale of inputs increase are matters of fact that depend upon production technology, they cannot be inferred from theory or discovered by some feat of imagination. A good rule of thumb is to expect constant returns to scale until some reason is discovered for expecting otherwise. It is possible to point to some common sources of increasing and decreasing returns to scale that are worth looking out for. They may have their origin in physical production or in the organisation of production.

Output may increase more than proportionately to inputs because production involves single acts, such as writing and editing the first copy of a newspaper or designing a new motor car, which do not need to be repeated as production continues. When inputs depend upon surface area and capacity depends upon volume, as in the pipes, cylinders and vats of breweries and chemical plant, inputs do not increase as fast as capacity. A third possibility is that production involves random variables. As the sample size of a random variable increases its variance about the mean decreases, and when inputs depend upon variance, as with stocks of spare parts, the law of large numbers may be associated with increasing returns to scale.

Looking beyond physical production there are possibilities of increasing returns from large organisations. Large organisations provide scope for managers with scarce talents, attract gifted management trainees, and retain large pools of candidates for

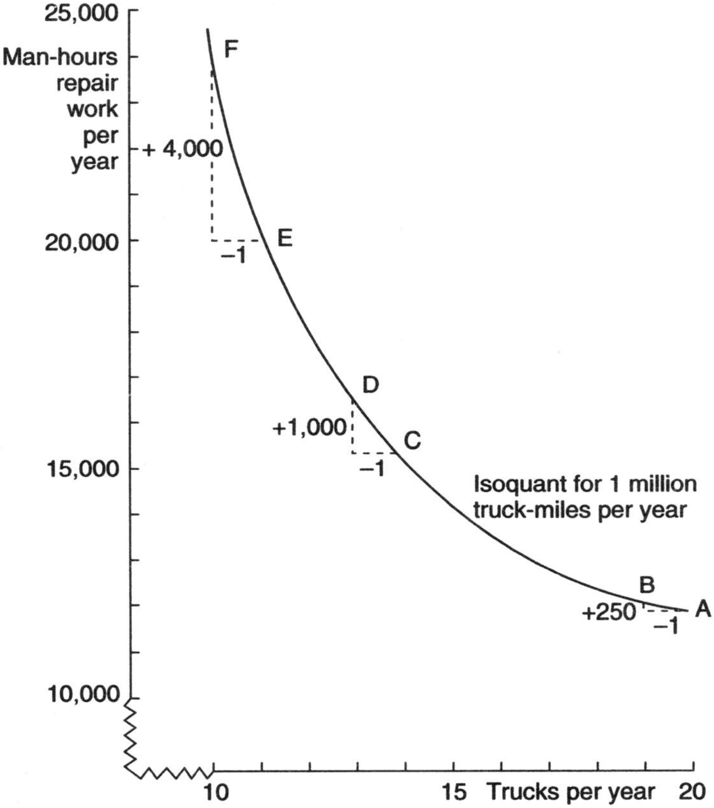

Figure 9.2 Substitution between mechanics and trucks

internal promotion. Large organisations are better able to face risks. Devotees of Damon Runyon will know that 'all life is six to five against', that the worst may happen. If it happens to a small firm that is generally the end, whilst a large company may have better things happening in one part to offset hardships in other parts. Less risk means greater availability of and lower rates for finance.

When increasing returns to large-scale organisation are added to those of large outputs it seems that everything favours the big battalions, and it often works out that way. Big can be beautiful. There are, however, some hazards of large organisations to be avoided.

As employment increases within a firm the number of possibilities for people to be at cross-purposes increases faster than the number of employees. Managers must be added to reconcile differences and secure unity of purpose. In a small firm an owner-manager can see what is going on in all parts of his business, and employees equally know where they fit in and what they are about. As a firm grows, functional specialists are appointed to manage aspects of the business, such as production, marketing and accounting. These specialists may see performance, pay and promotion in sectional terms: marketers seeking variety of product and rapid deliveries, production managers seeking standardisation, long runs and long lead times, and accountants seeking low stock costs even though stock-outs lose sales and impede production. Specialist managers must be managed. The outcome may be weakness in control, breakdowns in communication, and low morale.

There is therefore nothing sacrosanct about the straight slopes of vectors in Figure 9.1. If there are increasing returns to scale the slope of such vectors becomes progressively steeper; if there are decreasing returns the slopes get flatter as inputs increase. The implication for demand for inputs is that the effects of substituting between inputs may be offset or augmented by effects of the scale of production.

Diminishing returns

When output is increased by augmenting some, but not all, inputs, for simplicity augmenting one input and holding a second constant, the response of output to the varying input follows from the diminishing substitutability of one input for another. If one factor is increased it must be being called upon to make up for the lack of extra fixed factor. As factors differ from one another, that is, are not perfect substitutes, increasing a single input in a multi-factor production process must yield diminishing increments of output to equal additions of the variable factor. In terms of Figure 9.1, slopes such as AC and BC become flatter as one moves further and further from the axis of the fixed factor. This is the principle of diminishing returns, graced since the eighteenth century with the title of the Law of Diminishing Returns or, emphasising the changing mix of inputs, the Law of Variable Proportions.

3 MARKET CONSTRAINTS

The services of factors of production are not wanted for their own sake but for the revenue or, more immediately, the profit they provide. Demand for factors is derived from demand for products, and so product and factor markets must be considered together. The market structures examined in Part III, pure competition, monopoly and oligopoly, may be found in factor as well as product markets. Simply considering these three structures, there are nine combinations of factor and product markets: pure competition in factor market and pure competition in product market, pure competition in factor market and monopoly in product market, and so on. In addition it is necessary to look at the possibility of monopsony, a single buyer, in factor markets.

Fortunately, all the logical combinations of factor and product markets are not equally important. Pure competition predominates in factor markets. It is usual for large numbers of suppliers of factor services to face large numbers of buyers: materials, components and machinery are traded internationally, and men and women find work across a range of product markets. As argued earlier, the applicability of assumptions of pure competition widen in product markets when account is taken of potential competition. In this chapter attention is confined to pure competition in factor markets together with either pure competition or monopoly in product markets. Chapter 10 continues the discussion of competitive markets and restrictions within competitive markets. Monopoly and monopsony are given free rein in Chapter 11.

Profit maximisation

The marginal physical products of section 2 may be converted into marginal revenue products by multiplying product by marginal revenue. In pure competition marginal revenue equals product price, but care must be taken in choosing the price. When all competitive firms increase their use of a factor, output increases and product price falls. It is the product price associated with the output corresponding to factor usage which is relevant. Similarly, a monopolist must take account of the marginal revenue corresponding to changed factor use when multiplying marginal revenue, less than price, with marginal product.

It is evident that if the net revenue from employing an additional amount of a factor exceeds the increase in costs, profits must increase by employing the additional amount. Additional units should be employed so long as marginal net revenue exceeds marginal factor cost (in competitive factor markets, exceeds factor price), and hence maximum profits are attained when marginal net revenue equals marginal factor cost. This is the condition for maximising profits, equating marginal receipts with marginal costs, looked at from a different angle. Taking the competitive case and two inputs, X and Y, profit maximisation requires that for each factor marginal revenue multiplied by marginal physical product equals the price of the factor:

$$MR.MP_x = p_x$$
$$MR.MP_y = p_y$$

Dividing these two equations:

$$\frac{MR.MP_x}{MR.MP_y} = \frac{MP_x}{MP_y} = \frac{p_x}{p_y}$$

This is the condition relevant to the road transport example in section 2. The two equations may also be used to give:

$$MR = \frac{P_x}{MP_x} = \frac{P_y}{MP_y}$$

The amount of X needed to increase output by one unit is $1/MP_x$, and thus P_x $(1/MP_x)$ equals marginal cost.

It may be objected that businessmen do not think in this way; but it is not difficult to translate the argument into familiar terms.

Eight steps to factor demand

The calculation of the marginal net revenue of a factor may be divided into seven steps, one of which takes account of technology, four take account of product markets, one takes account of markets for substitutable or complementary inputs, and the seventh gives the marginal net revenue:

1. *Technology* Determine by how much the physical volume of production will increase if employment of a particular factor is increased slightly. Call the increase in amount the factor's marginal physical product. It is up to the management to decide whether to confine attention to one input or to consider all

inputs over its chosen planning period. A factor's marginal physical product is a technological fact.

2. *Product markets* Determine the selling price at which the marginal physical product may be sold. This is given by the market in competitive conditions but involves a market estimate.
3. Multiply the marginal physical product by the selling price to obtain the value of the marginal physical product.
4. If the firm has any perceptible influence on product price, determine whether the output originally produced must be sold at a lower price because of the firm's increased marginal production. Multiply any price reduction by the original output to obtain the revenue loss on sales because of the price cut.
5. Deduct any revenue loss on sales from the value of the marginal physical product to obtain the marginal gross revenue product.
6. *Substitutes and complements* When one factor replaces another, or when all factors are increased together, account must be taken of the prices of complementary or substitutable means of production. Determine whether the production of the marginal physical product involves increased or decreased outlays for other factors (materials, components, labour, machinery, and so on) and call such outlays associated expenses.
7. *Marginal net revenue product* Deduct the associated expenses from the marginal gross revenue product to obtain the marginal net revenue product.
8. *Factor demand* Increase employment of a factor so long as its marginal net revenue product exceeds its price.

Elasticity of factor demand

The eight steps indicate the forces affecting the responsiveness of the quantity demanded of a factor's services to changes in its price: technology, market opportunities, and supply conditions of complementary and substitutable inputs.

The greater the ease of substituting one input for another the more extensive are its possible uses should its price fall. The greater the substitutability of a factor the slower will returns diminish with increased input. Skilled workers, such as computer programmers, have no close substitutes and so are in inelastic demand, whereas unskilled assembly-line workers may be replaced by machinery and so are in elastic demand.

The more elastic the demand for the product the greater the response of sales to a reduction in product price associated with a lower factor price. Hence the more elastic is demand for a product the more elastic is demand for the means of its production.

Thirdly, market conditions in the supply of substitutes and complements must be taken into account. Suppose that X is substituted for Y following a fall in the price of X. If Y should be in inelastic supply, its price would fall as substitution takes place and the substitution process would be reduced in extent. If the increased use of a factor following a fall in its price involves complementary factors in inelastic supply, extension in its use will be inhibited by the rise in associated expenses.

Sections 2 and 3 have shown how profits and production, factor payments and productivity go together so that in competitive markets the prices of factors measure the value of their marginal products. The significance of factor prices as a measure may be seen by looking at the effects of the international mobility of factors of production.

4 INTERNATIONAL MOVEMENT OF FACTORS OF PRODUCTION

Economic activities become visible at political boundaries and are recorded by customs officials and border guards; but they are seldom seen from more than one side, although not always the same side. When scientists, engineers and other professional people emigrate they are most often seen as departing producers and not as departing income receivers and consumers. On the other hand, when multinationals enter the country they are most often seen as income receivers and not as output producers. Yet in each case salary or profit provides a measure of the marginal revenue product of the services withdrawn or introduced, so that, whilst the movement of people or capital is presumably to the advantage of those choosing the moves, it cannot have much effect on the economic well-being of those staying put.

The brain drain

Views on the international movement of highly trained and gifted people are often one-sided in a literal sense, concern being aroused when such people leave but no notice being taken when they return, more experienced and possibly better qualified, after a period abroad, and no notice being taken of foreign professionals who come as immigrants. In the decade 1973–82 on average 62,000 professional people emigrated from the United Kingdom each year and immigration averaged 47,000, so that there was a net annual loss of 15,000. These were professional people of all kinds, qualified in medicine and education as well as science and technology. There are roughly 500,000 scientists and engineers in Britain, a pool of talent which is augmented each year by new graduates and depleted by those retiring and emigrating. What would be the economic effect if 25,000 should choose to emigrate?

The answer frequently given is to take the salary of emigrants as a measure of their productivity, say £30,000 per year, and multiply by the number leaving, giving a loss of £750 million per year. This is clearly wrong. If the scientists and engineers stayed at home they and their families would consume the income, consumption offsetting production. There is not an exact offset, however, for two reasons.

First, the loss of production is greater than calculated. If 25,000 emigrated, the marginal revenue product of those remaining would rise as production adjusted to changing factor proportions and prices rose in affected product markets. A more exact calculation of the loss of output may be obtained using the theory of demand for factor services. The situation is illustrated in Figure 9.3 which shows the demand curve for services of scientists and engineers. The demand curve measures the marginal revenue product at each number of man-years so that the area under the demand curve between 475,000 and 500,000 man-years measures the full loss of output. The salaries of £30,000 multiplied by 25,000 is represented by the rectangle ABCD. The additional loss of output is represented by the triangle BEC, and this sum may be calculated if we know the elasticity of demand for professional services. BC=25,000, BE may be calculated, and the area BEC = (BC × BE)/2. For instance, if the elasticity of demand has an absolute value of 0.8:

$$0.8 = \frac{\text{percentage change in quantity demanded}}{\text{percentage change in price}}$$

$$= \frac{25{,}000/500{,}000}{\text{BE}/\pounds 30{,}000}$$

BE would equal £1,875 and BEC would equal £23.4 million. This would be the true dead-weight loss of the emigration, not £750

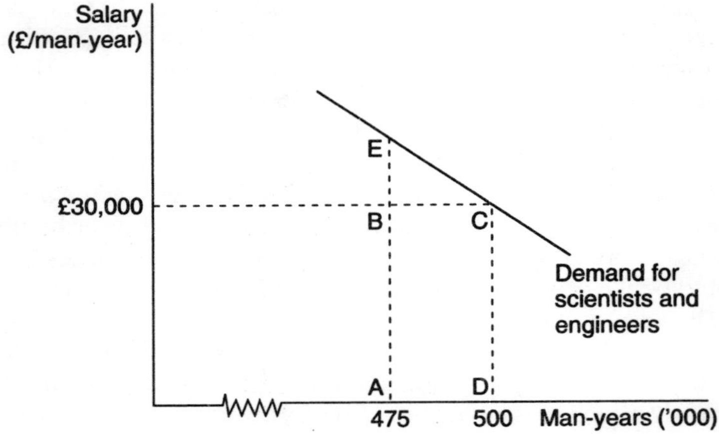

Figure 9.3 Effects of the brain drain

million. If the elasticity of demand is 0.5, the loss works out as £37.5 million; and if elasticity is 1.0, the loss is £18.8 million. The dead-weight loss of output is a modest sum at any likely elasticity of demand.

The second qualification is that scientists and engineers do not have the opportunity to consume their entire incomes. They must pay taxes, and when these taxes exceed direct benefits received from public expenditure there is a loss of taxes to be made good by taxpayers remaining at home. The redistributive element in taxation is difficult to calculate as it depends upon the size and age-structure of families; but the excess of taxes over benefits for emigrants would be likely to be £1,000–2,000 per head, and so tax loss would be of similar magnitude to the net loss of production. The total economic loss from emigration would still fall far short of salaries multiplied by numbers emigrating.

Multinationals

Analysis of the economic effects of multinational companies on host countries is similar to that of emigration, but in this case we have to consider an increase in the services of capital instead of a decrease in the services of highly skilled labour. Once more it must be remembered that British companies operate abroad (principally

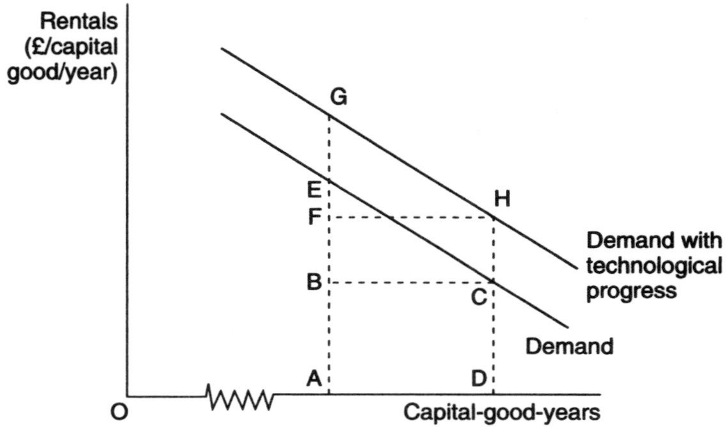

Figure 9.4 Multinational companies

in North America and Europe) as well as foreign multinationals in Britain. The scale of operations is similar in each direction and is considerable, foreign multinationals accounting for about 15 per cent of investment in British manufacturing.

The effects of incoming investment may be seen with the aid of Figure 9.4 which shows two demand curves for the services of capital goods, one assuming that incoming investment is of the same productivity as domestic capital and one assuming that multinationals introduce advanced technology and know-how. Once more, income payments, rentals of capital goods, offsets the value of changed production, but in this case there is a net gain in the value of production indicated by the triangles BEC and FGH beneath the demand curves. If the new investment brings improved technology, the net gain may increase or the additional product may accrue as additional profits to foreign shareholders. Tax considerations are more important when considering investment. The gain to domestic taxpayers is likely to be greater in this case because business taxes bear no relationship to the public services provided for companies.[2]

Economic benefits and detriments do not exhaust the questions raised by emigration or multinationals. The theory of demand for factor services does suggest, however, that strong economic arguments about international factor mobility are suspect.

5 SUMMARY

- The theory of demand for the services of factors of production is based upon profit maximisation in individual firms. In order to maximise profit inputs must be adjusted so that marginal revenue product per unit of input equals marginal factor cost. In competitive markets, marginal factor cost is the same as factor price, and hence in equilibrium factor price provides a measure of marginal revenue product.
- Demand reflects both technological constraints on production and marketing opportunities for output. Changing factor proportions by substituting inputs at constant levels of output or increasing some inputs whilst holding others constant involves diminishing rates of substitution or diminishing returns. These may be affected by economies or diseconomies of scale.
- In competitive product markets demand for inputs is the sum of demands of individual firms and must take account of product prices associated with combined outputs. In monopolised product markets a firm must take account of changing marginal revenue as output changes.
- The elasticity of demand for a factor depends upon its substitutability for other inputs, the behaviour of other factor prices and elasticity of supply of these other factors, and the elasticity of demand for the product.
- The fact that in competitive markets the demand price for a factor measures its marginal revenue product makes possible calculation of effects on the value of production caused by changes in factor supplies such as those brought about by international movement of labour and capital.

10

SUPPLY, SUPPLY AND DEMAND, AND RESTRICTED COMPETITION

1 INTRODUCTION

There is no single theory of factor supply corresponding to the marginal productivity theory of factor demand. Raw materials, components, tools and machines are all provided by product markets and their supply is determined by the forces considered in Part III. The most important input, however, is human effort and this calls for special consideration as it has to be supplied in person. Firms wish to buy personal services but services and servant go together. This makes labour markets different from other markets. The supply of labour is examined in the next section. Supply and demand are put together in section 3 to help unravel a mediaeval mystery. Section 4 also uses supply and demand theory to analyse the efficiency of factor markets when there are restrictions on competition. This section is devoted to colour bars and sex equality, and to the reasons why trade unionists may be closet racists and sexists whilst capitalists seem colour-blind.

2 WHEN AND WHERE TO WORK

Men and women do not decide separately how much and what kind of effort to supply; but the decision process is easier to understand if it is broken into stages. First, there is the decision about how long to work.

Participation

In the United Kingdom, out of a population of almost 58 million,

28 million actively seek paid employment. The rest are either growing up, bringing up families, or growing old. Three out of four men aged 16 and over were economically active in 1991, the highest rate in the European community. Activity rates for men, the percentage of an age-group in or seeking work, vary from 95 per cent for 35-44 year olds down to 8 per cent for those over 60 years. These rates have been changing markedly since the Second World War as youths have stayed on in higher education and men have retired at earlier ages. Activity rates for women also vary, being high among young women, lower during child-bearing years, and high once more in middle age. The biggest change has been in the activity rates for wives, which has more than doubled to 50 per cent.

Nearly one-half of women and one-fifteenth of men work part-time, mainly from choice; but the difference between part-time and full-time is only the largest of many differences in working hours. About one-half of men working full-time work a 40-hour week, some of the remainder work shorter hours but most work longer, one-third of them very much longer. It is not the case that people are obliged to work a standard working week.[1]

Income v. leisure

Economic analysis of the supply of hours of work is based on Disraeli's dictum that 'increased means and increased leisure are the two civilizers of man'. Men and women are seen as desiring both more income to spend and more time in which to spend it. They may trade leisure for income on terms dictated by the wage-rate, and seek an optimum position where the marginal rate of substitution between leisure and income equals the hourly wage-rate. If the wage-rate is £7 per hour more hours will be offered so long as an extra hour of leisure is valued at less than £7. The decision may be illustrated using indifference curves.

In Figure 10.1, hours per week are measured along the horizontal axis, leisure hours rightwards from the origin and working hours leftwards from A. Weekly income is measured along the vertical axis. In a typical week a worker spends 24 hours on essential activities, such as cooking, shopping, child care, eating meals, washing, getting up and going to bed, and 56 hours sleeping: this leaves 88 hours for employment and other activities. OA thus represents 88 hours.

At A, many people have some income whether they work or

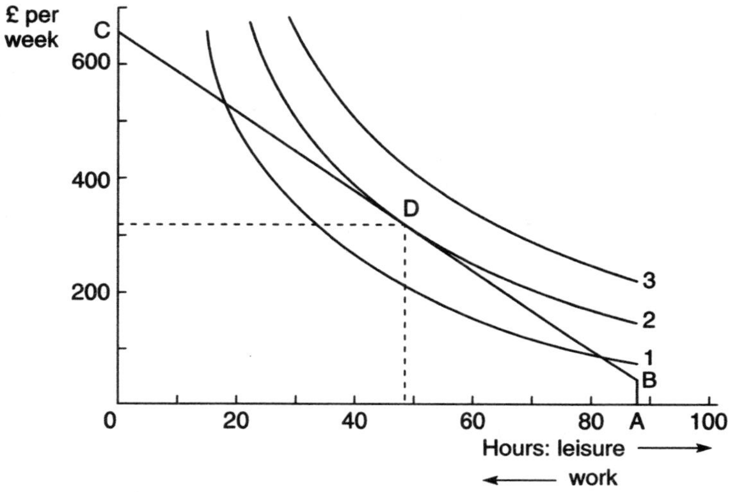

Figure 10.1 Work v. leisure

not: it may be the earnings of husband or wife, social security benefits or income from interest or dividends, although some start the week in a negative position with obligations to meet, such as hire-purchase payments. In Figure 10.1, the position is shown of someone enjoying £40 per week whether he works or not, and able to earn £7 per hour. His budget line runs from A to B (88 hours leisure and £40 income) to C (88 hours work and £656 income), and his optimum choice is at D where he reaches the highest indifference curve attainable, working 40 hours for £280 and enjoying 48 hours leisure with a total income of £320.

Equilibrium positions such as D are of little interest in themselves, but gain importance as starting points for analysis of what happens when some condition changes. In the present case it is possible to derive an individual's supply curve of labour by varying the wage-rate. Changes in the wage-rate pivot the budget line around B, the line getting steeper for increases in the wage-rate and flatter for reductions. Figure 10.2 traces the effect of an increase in the wage-rate which shifts the budget line from ABC to ABE. It can be seen that hours of work supplied may increase from AK to AM as in (i), decrease from AK to AM as in (ii), or remain

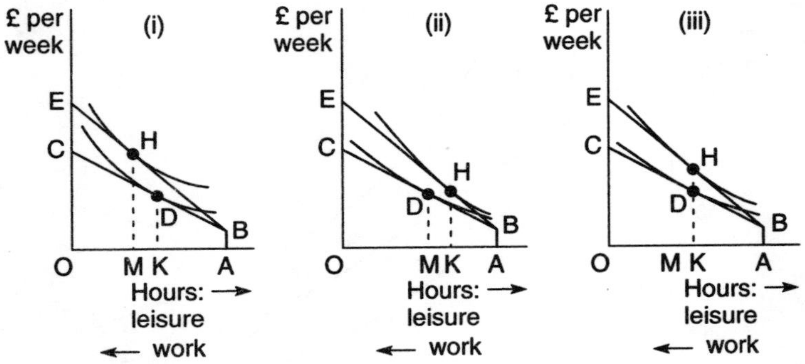

Figure 10.2 Three possibilities

unchanged at AK as in (iii). The three possibilities mean that the actual response to an increase in the wage-rate must be investigated and cannot be deduced from pure theory, still less from personal prejudice.

The response of workers to wage-rates is a matter about which strong opinions are often held. Colonial administrators and employers often believed that natives would work less hard if they were paid more, although there was no evidence for such a belief. In developed countries, conviction politicians often argue that taxes must be reduced to give people an incentive to work harder, although there is considerable evidence that reduced rates of taxes on income (equivalent to an increase in the wage-rate) have little, if any, effect on hours worked, and the effect may be up or down. Taxpayers do not, of course, need the prospect of a spur to further effort in order to see the desirability of reduced taxes.[2]

It is likely that poorly paid workers will wish to work longer hours when wage-rates are increased, and well-paid workers to work unchanged or fewer hours. The reason is best seen by looking more closely at the case where an individual chooses to work fewer hours when the wage-rate is increased. This is illustrated in Figure 10.3. The effect of increasing the wage-rate and shifting the budget line from ABC to ABE is that the terms of exchange between income and leisure are changed, leisure becoming more expensive in terms of income forgone, and a whole new range of possibilities of improved real income, which may be taken in increased purchasing power or greater leisure, are opened up.

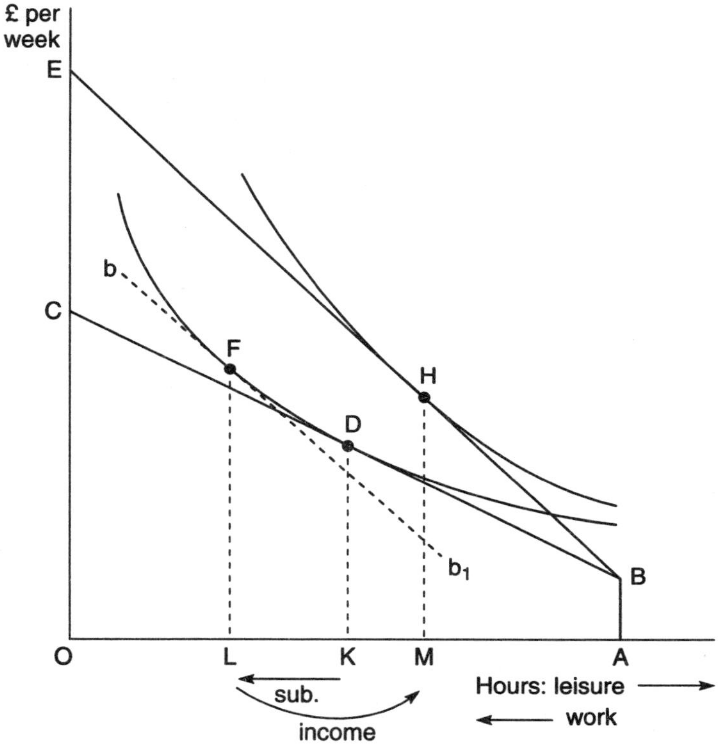

Figure 10.3 Substitution and income effects

These two effects may be separated by enquiring what the effect would be of offering the improved wage-rate but simultaneously reducing the individual's initial income so that he is held at the original real income depicted by indifference curve 1. The effect is shown by the dashed budget line bb_1. The optimum position moves from D to F, the hours that would be worked increasing from AK to AL. This is the substitution effect of an increase in the wage-rate, and it would always unequivocally lead to an increase in hours worked. If the initial income is now restored the eventual equilibrium is attained at H, hours of work actually falling from AK to AM. The move from F to H, involving a reduction in hours of work of LM, is termed the income effect of the change in wage-rate. As leisure is a normal good, more being demanded when income increases, the income effect is always to reduce the number of hours of work chosen.

The outcome therefore depends upon the relative size of the substitution and income effects. When the substitution effect is larger than the income effect, working hours chosen increase; when the substitution effect is smaller than the income effect, working hours fall; and when the two effects offset one another the disposition of time does not change. The income effect is likely to be small relative to the substitution effect at low rates of wages when the greatest need is for increased purchasing power, and to be large at high rates of wages when time is needed to enjoy purchasing power. An individual's supply curve of working hours may therefore have an upward-sloping section at low wages and a backward-bending section at high wages.[3]

Industry supply

Backward-bending individual supply curves do not necessarily imply backward-sloping supply curves for an industry for two reasons. First, the point at which individual supply curves bend backwards may differ between workers so that when individual supplies are added together the total supply curve slopes upwards. Secondly, the group of firms supplying a particular product are unlikely to be the only employers of a particular kind of labour and so find that larger supplies of labour come forward at the higher wages needed to attract people from outside employers.

Non-pecuniary considerations: where to work

The possibility of working in different occupations brings forward considerations additional to hours worked and money received. As Adam Smith observes:

> Pecuniary wages and profit, indeed, are everywhere in Europe extremely different according to the different employments of labour and stock. But this difference arises partly from certain circumstances in the employment themselves, which, either really, or at least in the imaginations of men, make up for a small pecuniary gain in some, and counterbalance a greater one in others.[4]

Men and women generally prefer jobs that provide opportunities for the exercise of skill, growth of skill, autonomy, identification with the final product, friendly associates, agreeable surroundings, and so on. They are less attracted by dull, dirty, dangerous jobs. Women like jobs that start after schools open and end before schools close.

Factory work provides the satisfaction of making things in friendly surroundings that are often clean, light and pleasant. It may be simple work that becomes automatic and so lets people day-dream or chat to friends. On the other hand, factories can be hot or cold, noisy, dirty, greasy and depressing: the work is usually repetitive and may involve sitting or standing in the same place all day: and workers may never see the finished product. Computer operators work in an exciting, rapidly changing area, providing new challenges as equipment and techniques change, and one where there is plenty of freedom to change employer; but the concentration involved may be tiring, the equipment noisy, the air-conditioning and 'no-smoking' rules may be uncongenial to some, and shift-work uncongenial to others.

The provision of personal services also involves much more than hours of work and rates of pay. Professional footballers, for example, have a skilled, challenging, exciting and glamorous job which many regard as play rather than work and which takes them to distant, exotic places; but, looking on the other side, it is a hard, exhausting, competitive and insecure job often performed in foul conditions of mud, rain and snow; a place in the team may go because of loss of form or injury; non-playing days can be boring (alcoholism is said to be a problem); private lives are public property; there is much work away from home; and the average career lasts no more than ten years. Doctors have to weigh job satisfaction and social status on the one hand against long hours, night calls, unpleasant tasks, and stress and strain (alcoholism is once more a problem). It is well-known that 'a policeman's lot is not a happy one'.[5]

Decisions on how many hours of work to offer at a particular rate of pay are thus multi-dimensional, and supply curves of labour must be interpreted as making full allowance for non-pecuniary advantages and disadvantages. If there is a balance of advantage, the supply curve will be further to the right than would be the case if it only reflected monetary remuneration.

These supply considerations, together with the earlier analysis of factor demand and the working of product markets, may be put to work to unravel the mystery of population movements in the fourteenth century.

3 THE BLACK DEATH

Although the plague that reached England in 1348 and spread throughout 1349 did not become known as the Black Death until two hundred years after the event, there is no reason to doubt its deadliness. As one chronicler put it: 'It slew Jew, Christian and Saracen alike; it carried off confessor and penitent alike . . . It filled the whole world with terror.' No estimate of mortality rates falls below 250 per 1,000 and there is some evidence to suggest rates as high as 450 per 1,000. This compares with mortality rates of 40 per 1,000 for earlier years and present-day rates of 11–12 per 1,000. However, population is capable of rapid changes upwards as well as downwards so that the catastrophic death-toll implies nothing about subsequent population size.[6] So what did happen to the population?

There are no firm figures for the size of the population before censuses began to be taken in the nineteenth century. Historians base estimates on the Domesday Survey, 1086, and the Poll Tax Returns, 1377; but the former only provides information, with omissions, about heads of households, and the latter were subject to an uncertain amount of avoidance. This paucity of information about the size of the population contrasts with the amount of information on prices and wages paid from year to year by religious houses and colleges. M.M. Postan saw that this market information provided evidence of population changes.[7]

Records show that wages of agricultural workers rose throughout the century following the Black Death. Other things being equal, wages would rise if the supply of labour fell. The wage records may therefore provide evidence of changes in population; but only if other possible causes of the rise in wages can be eliminated. There are three such possibilities.

First, productivity could have improved so that an unchanged or increased number of workers would be employed at rising wages. Secondly, industrial expansion could have provided employment opportunities outside agriculture so that the supply of workers on farms could have fallen without the total population falling. Thirdly, money wages might have risen as a result of inflation.

An improvement in agricultural productivity may be eliminated on direct and indirect evidence. Output per acre did not increase despite the abandonment of marginal land, possibly because of a worsening climate. Furthermore, if the productivity of labour had increased, rents would have been maintained or increased and direct cultivation of demesne land would have remained profitable. Rents fell and lords of the manor cultivated less land themselves.

The second possibility, of industry attracting workers away from farms, may also be eliminated. Wages in woollen manufacture, clothing and building would have had to begin rising before agricultural wages; but in fact they rose at the same time as agricultural wages, although not to the same extent. Employment outside agriculture did not exceed 10 per cent of total employment, employment in woollen manufacture not more than 1 per cent, and so a large increase in manufacturing employment would have a very small effect on the supply of agricultural workers.

It seems strange to find monetarists arguing that wages rose because of an increase in the money supply some two centuries before the influx of silver from the New World. It is true that silver mines in central Europe were increasing their output; but there are many steps between an increase in mining output in central Europe and an increase in specie circulation in Britain, and these steps do not seem to have been taken. If the increase in wages were simply a monetary phenomenon, nominal wages would have increased but wages would not have increased in purchasing power. In fact wages rose when measured in grains of silver, bushels of wheat, or in power of purchasing a representative basket of goods.[8] Changes in real wages are not a monetary phenomenon.

The course of wages therefore provides evidence of a reduction in the supply of labour and thus of a reduction in population. Once Postan had established this, further pointers to a changing population were discovered. For instance, wages began rising before the Black Death and evidence was uncovered of starvation in the wet years of 1316 and 1317. Some abandoned villages discovered by aerial photography date from before the Black Death and are on such infertile land that it has never since seemed worth cultivating: people depending on it must have been very hungry. The virulence of the plague may therefore have worsened because the population was already in a weak state of health. Further evidence has accumulated since Postan made his original investigation, with population estimated to have moved in inverse pattern to real wages between 1250 and 1750.[9]

It is evident that anyone who believes that modern economics only applies to modern times is mistaken; but let us return to the present.

4 RACIST AND SEXIST DISCRIMINATION

Up to this point there has only been passing reference to the gender and no reference to the ethnic origin of wage-earners. It may seem to a member of the second sex in the Third World that insufficient attention has been paid to prejudice. Demand and supply analysis can throw some light on its operation, demonstrating why privileged workers and their trade unions rather than employers often prove the strongest supporters of racial or sexual discrimination, and why the same rate for the job irrespective of sex, colour or creed may be the means to employment discrimination. In the present context, discrimination means paying people less than their potential marginal revenue product: potential product may or may not equal actual product.

Racial discrimination

The effects of racial discrimination may be illustrated by the simplest case where members of two races could do each other's work. Figure 10.4 shows the situation in markets for semi-skilled and unskilled labour. In the absence of colour bars, the number of white workers seeking semi-skilled work is OA, the number of black workers AB: total employment is OB and the wage OC. OH black workers are employed in unskilled work at a wage of OJ. If occupations are segregated so that only whites may hold semi-skilled jobs and blacks must all work in the unskilled area, the wages of whites will rise and the wages of blacks fall. Output equal to the area ADEB which would be the product of black workers in semi-skilled jobs is lost, and black workers are only able to add to output GHKL in unskilled work: black wages are OM per worker, below the wage they might earn in the absence of segregation, and the contribution blacks make to total production is less than it otherwise might be. Wages of whites are ON instead of OC.

The fact pointed out by some welfare economists that black workers could afford to bribe white workers to let them work in semi-skilled jobs, making everyone better-off in material terms, shows the limitations of such compensation tests. It should come

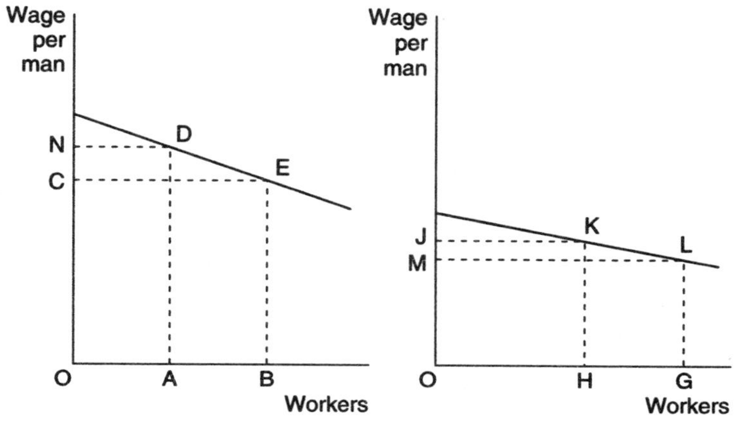

(a) Semi-skilled work

(b) Unskilled work

Figure 10.4 Effects of colour bars

as no surprise that white trade unionists have been among the strongest supporters of demarcations, and that employers, such as the Anglo-American Group in South Africa, should have been amongst opponents. Apartheid meant that employers could not take advantage of the fact that black wages were held below potential marginal revenue product. It needs no great mathematical ability to see that potential profits go begging whilst potential marginal revenue product is less than marginal factor cost. When profits are not involved colour prejudice has free rein. Liverpool has had a coloured community for over a century, but until recently the local authority has had the worst reputation for discrimination in the city.

This argument is based on the assumption that members of privileged and underprivileged groups are of equal productivity, an assumption that is realistic if attention is concentrated on low levels of skill but not otherwise. Discrimination in employment usually follows unequal access to education and training, so that members of privileged and unprivileged groups cannot be expected usually to be of equal productivity. It is no kindness to the underprivileged in such circumstances to suggest that they should be paid at the same rates as the privileged. This is a point which many well-intentioned people miss. They wish unemployment or confinement to unskilled jobs on the underprivileged by advocating equal pay when the underprivileged cannot offer equal work. The fact that discrimination may take the form of unemployment rather than unequal payment for equal work may be seen in the area where it is perilous to suggest unequal productivity: sexual discrimination.

Sexual discrimination

The Equal Pay Act was passed in 1970 and came into effect in 1975: it provided that women within the same firm were to receive equal treatment with men (a) on work of the same or broadly similar nature, and (b) in jobs that, though different from those of men, were of equal value. In 1970, hourly wage-rates of women were 83 per cent of those of men and in 1980 equalled those of men, hourly earnings were 64 per cent of men and in 1980 were 71 per cent, and the ratio of female employment to male employment increased from 40 per cent in 1970 and 46 per cent in 1980. Did this mean that sexual equality had broken out in Britain?

In order to answer this question it is necessary to distinguish income discrimination from employment discrimination. Figures 10.5(a) and (b) depict the marginal revenue productivity of female labour as seen by an objective observer, say an asexual Martian, by DD_o, and the demand curve operating in the market by DD_m. The difference between an objective view of female productivity and a management view of such productivity might be explained by managers all being male chauvinist pigs; but unanimity is essential. If one manager recognised that the market was underestimating female productivity, he could get ahead of his rivals by employing more women. Unanimous male attitudes are more easily recognised by women than by men. Alternatively, male workers may refuse to accept the equality of women so that their potential productivity is never allowed demonstration, or customers may be prejudiced so that, although a Martian could recognise that a female engineer, lawyer, doctor, judge, sales representative, electrician, taxicab driver or security officer is quite as productive as a male, employers are obliged to go along with their customers.

Two possibilities emerge. Women might be paid less than men, and so less than their potential marginal revenue productivity. This is shown in Figure 10.5(a). The supply of female labour is SS. As women are potentially as productive as men, if there were no

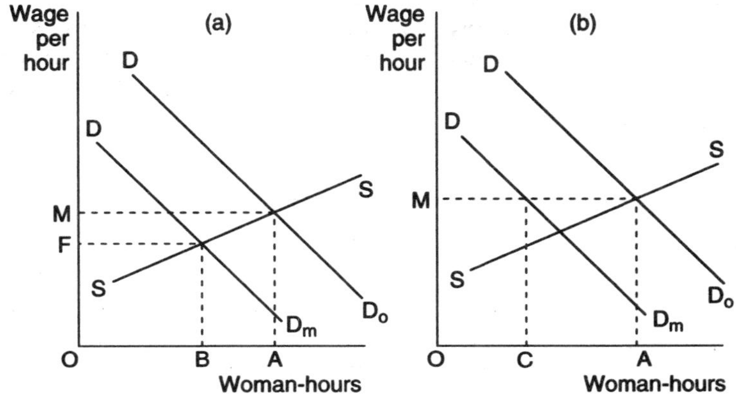

(a) Wage discrimination (b) Employment discrimination

Figure 10.5

discrimination their wages would be at the male level OM and female employment would be OA. Discrimination means that they are paid OF, below their potential productivity, and employment is OB. Alternatively, women could be paid at the same rate as men but fewer would be employed. This is illustrated in Figure 10.5(b). Women receive the male wage OM but only OC are employed. Once more the female wage is below potential productivity, and those prevented by wage equality from being employed at a lower wage must crowd into occupations at still lower wages.

In order for the Equal Pay Act to be seen to be working it is therefore necessary for the rate of pay of women to increase after the Act, and also for the ratio of female to male employment to be maintained or increased. The statistics quoted earlier therefore seem a triumphant vindication of the Equal Pay Act: relative pay of women has increased and so has their employment. Unfortunately, all theoretical arguments are subject to the proviso, 'other things being equal'. In the 1970s employment in the public sector, where there was no sex discrimination, grew so that hourly earnings of women relative to men would have increased had there been no Equal Pay Act. In other occupations female employment fell, and so it seems likely that in some occupations employment discrimination took the place of pay discrimination. Employment discrimination is to be found where women, although paid the same as men, occupy positions for which they are over-qualified. It is also present when men occupy all the senior positions despite the presence of women with equal qualifications and equal length of service.

5 SUMMARY

- Men and women decide how many hours to work by balancing the attractions of larger money income against hours in which to enjoy money income.
- A higher hourly rate of pay improves the terms on which money income may be substituted for leisure, but also increases the money income provided by all levels of effort. An individual will work longer hours if the substitution effect is greater than the income effect; but if his income is not below the average level, the substitution and income effects are likely to offset one another.
- The fact that individuals may choose to work shorter hours at higher rates of pay does not mean that the supply curve of labour to an industry will be backward sloping: individuals' supply curves may bend backwards at different levels of wages, and workers may need attracting from other industries.
- Money and hours are only two items in an employment contract: non-pecuniary advantages and disadvantages also need taking into account.
- Demand and supply analysis offers four possible reasons for a rise in money wages: physical productivity may have improved, the relative price of the product may have increased, the rise may be merely nominal resulting from inflation, or the supply of labour may have fallen. If the first three reasons do not apply, the explanation must be a fall in the supply of labour. *Memento mori.*
- Racial discrimination reduces total output and profits below their potential level; but makes possible higher wages for the privileged groups. Colour bars are therefore often supported by workers and opposed by capitalists.
- Unequal treatment of workers may take the form of paying some less than others for equal work, or paying all the same but restricting employment of the underprivileged.

11

MARKET COMPLICATIONS: INFORMATION, CO-OPERATION AND CONFLICT

1 INTRODUCTION

Every effort has been made in the last two chapters to keep flesh and blood in mind; but the analysis may have seemed a shade mechanical. Men and women have to take market forces into account, but they do not react like automatons to the market. In the first place, they have to discover what their employment opportunities are. Secondly, they and their employers have to find ways of working together so that product and payments are maximised. Thirdly, they need to take account of conflicts of interests as well as complementary interests.

Section 2 considers the difficulties faced by workers and employers in securing enough information about each other's performance, and the consequences for labour markets. After matching work and worker, employment relationships for adults are fairly stable. In Great Britain, 85–90 per cent of workers remain with the same employer from one year to the next. The complementary interests of the two sides of industry, given scope within internal labour markets, form the subject of section 3. Industrial conflict is considered in the fourth section.

2 IMPERFECT INFORMATION

Search

Demand and supply diagrams picture a situation where a regular flow of man-hours is provided by workers and made use of by employers who have somehow met and contracted with one another. In reality workers must find a job and are on the look-out for better jobs and employers have to recruit as well as retain employees. Labour contracts are typically open-ended. A worker agrees to accept the authority of management in return for a wage. He therefore needs information about the nature of the management, working practices, working conditions, opportunities for training, promotion and so on, in addition to the wage offered.

The need for job search explains one element of unemployment, frictional unemployment, found in employment equilibria. If demand were sufficient to provide work for everyone, with numbers joining the market equalling those leaving, there would still be a pool of people looking for work. The pool swells when demand falls and dwindles as demand picks up but it cannot dry up entirely. Job search helps explain the number of changes made by young entrants to the labour market as they seek work that suits them best, and employers discover their qualities. It helps explain the persistence of a range of wage payments in the same occupation for workers of similar ability. It is not worth while to keep on looking for ever for the best-paying employer or the cheapest employee.

Looking for work is more stressful than looking for a best buy, and the process of job search differs in other respects from that of product search considered in Chapter 8. In that chapter attention was paid to finding the best buy in a fixed sample size: as search proceeded the chances of finding a better buy fell and the probable size of any improvement fell, but having searched a customer could make the best purchase that had been uncovered. Job search is sequential, and if an opportunity is not taken up it is likely to be lost for ever.

Consider someone looking for work. The first job offered may be accepted, but if it is rejected it is no longer available. As the quest proceeds it is possible to rank the jobs discovered. The aim is to find the best vacancy. In order to keep the argument simple, suppose that there are only four vacancies, A, B, C and D, which are ranked in that order after their good and bad points have been discovered. There are 24 ways in which these vacancies might be found:

ABC(D)	ABD(C)	AC(B)D	ACD(B)	AD(B)C
AD(C)B	B(A)CD	B(A)DC	BC(A)D	BCD(A)
BD(A)C	BD(C)A	C(A)BD	C(A)DB	C(B)AD
C(B)DA	CD(A)B	CD(B)A	D(A)BC	D(A)CB
D(B)AC	D(B)CA	D(C)AB	D(C)BA	

If the first vacancy is taken there are 18 chances of missing the best job, and six chances of finishing with the worst of the four. If the entire field is reviewed, the chances are the same. It should be possible to do better.

If the job-seeker rejects the first vacancy encountered and accepts the first job after that which ranks higher than its predecessor, the possible outcomes are those bracketed above. It will be seen that the worst job is chosen in only one case, there are five possibilities of choosing C, eight chances of finding B, and ten chances of finding A. If the first two vacancies are passed over and a vacancy ranking higher than its predecessor is then chosen, the searcher would be left with D in two more cases, the chance of C would be unchanged, B would be chosen in seven instead of eight, and A in nine instead of ten. In this example, where there are no costs of search, it pays to search but not to search too much. Sequential search increases knowledge but opportunities are sacrificed as knowledge improves. The general rule where there are larger numbers of vacancies to consider is, according to J.A. Paulos, to reject the first 37 per cent of vacancies and choose the first job then ranking higher than its predecessor.[1]

This rule needs modifying when the costs of job search are taken into account. Workers consult friends and relatives, keep an eye on newspaper advertisements, look out for notices at works' entrances, make use of employment exchanges and employment agencies, make applications and travel to interviews. It all takes time and often costs money directly. It always costs money indirectly in that income is forgone whilst search continues. Search is worth while so long as the gain in present value from future employment exceeds the cost.

Signalling and screening

In order to bring the search process to an end applicants have to successfully signal to employers their suitability for a job and employers have to screen applicants to identify the most suitable. One signal and screen is educational attainment. Irrespective of what is learned, commitment to study shows self-discipline, ambition, application and ability to take a long view. It therefore makes sense for an employer to pay attention to levels of education. The efficiency of educational attainment as a screen depends upon the ease of access to education and its even quality. The screening could have a self-selection element as the less able opt out of education, finding qualifications hard to acquire and the uncertain prospect of future gain in income an insufficient offset against the present hardship of study.

Larger lifetime income is closely correlated with higher educational attainment. When differences in income are compared with the costs of extra education in the form of income forgone, fees, books and equipment, the private returns on investment in education are high. A bachelor's degree typically returns about 10 per cent.[2] The social return is lower: the cost borne by taxpayers is offset to varying degrees by the higher taxes paid by graduates. Investment in human capital has provided an effective, though philistine, support for increased public expenditure on education. Extreme exponents of the screening hypothesis argue that educational qualifications are simply tickets to lush jobs where people can exert their innate abilities. Whatever has been learnt during education is an irrelevance. There is, of course, no reason why education should not be seen as preparing people for work as well as opening up opportunities for work.

The allocation of workers to jobs and the determination of their rates of pay is completed at the port of entry for small firms and those offering temporary work or jobs requiring little skill; but a large workforce gives an employer the opportunity to take over from the external market, training people in special skills and ways of working, filling vacancies beyond the entry level by internal promotion, offering a career rather than a single job, and agreeing a wage and salary structure to suit the organisation's specific purposes.

3 INTERNAL LABOUR MARKETS

An internal labour market cannot be divorced entirely from demand and supply in the outside world. New employees are recruited from outside and insiders must be provided with conditions that compare well with those outside; but personnel administrators can add their own influence to the background market forces. Japanese companies symbolise membership of internal labour markets by having everyone dress in the same company uniform, but large British companies differ sartorially much more than in substance.

General and specific training

Low labour turnover helps overcome problems of training and retraining. Skills usually have two components, enhanced knowledge and ability that has general use and some that is specific to particular employment, for example, the ability to fly an aircraft and the ability to fly Concorde.

General training is usually paid for by the trainee in fees and income forgone and is sometimes financed by taxpayers. Firms are in a prisoners' dilemma regarding such training. All firms in an industry gain from better-trained workers well grounded in their technologies. If they all provide general training they all enjoy improved productivity; but any firm opting out could poach workers and enjoy the productivity at competitors' cost, and as this applies to all they are all likely to opt out and all finish worse off. General training was traditionally provided by firms to apprentices who paid for their own training by working for low wages during the period of apprenticeship.

Specific training raises fewer problems and is well suited to an internal labour market. Training in the special methods, routines and equipment used by a firm must be provided within the firm: part is provided formally and part gained from learning on the job. The cost of such training may be partly borne by trainees in the form of lower wages during training, or may be fully met by the employer paying the going wage during training and recouping from the greater product of the trained worker. Investment in human capital is made for a return that should be comparable to a firm's other investment, and this return depends on creating a long-term employment relationship.

Job ladders

Undertaking specific training gives workers an incentive to remain with their employers because their enhanced productivity is lost if they move back into the external labour market. This incentive is reinforced in some industries such as oil refining, steel and rail transport by the provision of job ladders that workers can climb as they learn on the job and gain experience on each rung of the ladder.

In the absence of formal job ladders, firms are still likely to prefer promoting from within their own workforce rather than bringing in outsiders to fill more senior posts. Promotion prospects are good for morale and provide an incentive to work well without constant supervision. Internal promotion is also more efficient in that there is always a lot more known about the character and abilities of insiders than can be gained from taking references and interviewing outsiders.

Principals and agents

The advantages of an internal labour market may be summed up as a solution to the principal–agent problem of securing mutuality of interests between those providing work and those performing it. Loyalty is built up by creating conditions in which people can earn more by staying put than they could earn elsewhere. Productivity is augmented by training, and with reduced costs of monitoring and supervision net marginal revenue products are further increased. The payment of higher wages than those in the outside market becomes both possible and profitable.

A more cynical view is that firms pay 'efficiency wages' that are higher than those needed to recruit from outside in order to increase employees' fear of being thrown out into the cold. The penalty for shirking is increased and marginal products levered above those of outside workers. The wage provides the productivity rather than the productivity the wage. If all firms pursue such a policy they are seen to produce a reserve army of unemployed who serve by standing and waiting. This could happen if the unemployed do not provide lower-cost labour to emerging competitors; but it seems unlikely.

Internal markets are a means of reconciling the interests of employer and employee. They may, however, be a cause of conflict if they create a market structure of bilateral monopoly with a single purchaser (monopsonist) facing a trade union representing all the employees (monopolist). Monopsony and monopoly may also cause problems in the external labour market.

4 MONOPSONY AND MONOPOLY

In the last two chapters account has been taken of monopoly in the product market but not in the sale of factor services and no attention has been paid to monopsony in the purchase of services. Suppliers of factor services have faced external and internal market prices. They have not had the opportunity to agree jointly on the price or to limit entry so as to raise the price. Purchasers have not needed to take account of their individual influence on the price of services bought: they too have faced going market prices.

Monopsony

Monopsony – a single employer or a group of employers acting together – could be seen operating in the football league until the agreement to limit the maximum wage clubs could pay was found to be a restraint of trade. Footballers' wages were limited to about three times the average manual wage. This exercise of monopoly hiring power, however, had special features. The clubs were far from profit maximisers, being content at best with breaking even, and the effect of the wage restriction was to share the rent of ability of star players amongst their team-mates and prevent large clubs from recruiting all the best players. It was clearly against the interests of star players but may not have been against the well-being of the game.

Monopsony power could also be seen in action in the size of fees offered by the BBC for sporting spectacles when it was the sole television broadcaster. The increased fees offered by independent companies raised a cheer from sports fans, but since satellite companies began offering sport on pay-as-you-view terms they may once more be tempted to nostalgia for good old monopsony days.

There is no cause for sentimentality about the general case of monopsony in a labour market where a profit-maximising firm is the only source of employment. This may be the situation of immobile workers, such as housewives, or of immigrants with language problems. As Figure 11.1 shows, a monopsonist needs to take account of the increase in the wage-rate that has to be paid to attract more recruits. Instead of equating marginal revenue product with the supply price of labour, marginal revenue product is equated with the marginal cost of labour. The wage paid, AB, is less than the marginal revenue product, AC. This is economically inefficient in that the value of extra product from additional employment exceeds its cost depicted by the supply curve of labour. If a minimum wage were imposed at a level above AB, the value of output and level of employment would rise.

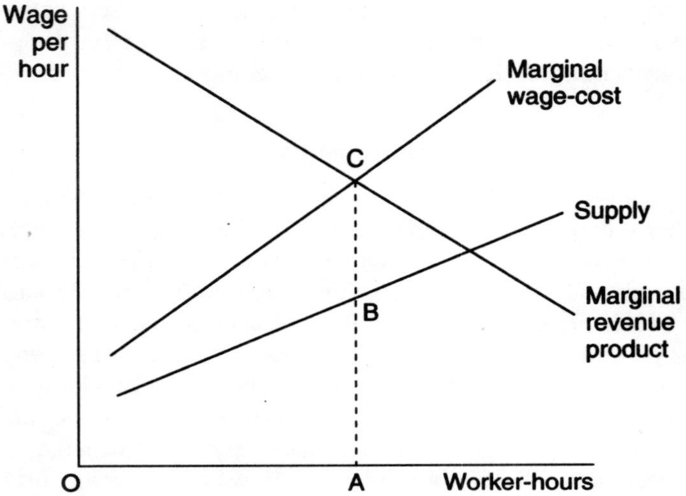

Figure 11.1 Monopsony in the labour market

Monopoly

The monopolistic supplier of a service intent on the highest reward needs to take account of the decline in marginal revenue product with increased labour input. Income is maximised when the marginal supply price equals the rate of change in marginal revenue product. This is shown in Figure 11.2 where the wage equals DF when marginal supply price equals marginal revenue to the supplier at E. Once more potential surplus EFG is lost and employment restricted.

The wage DF could be achieved by suppliers of a service agreeing to this level of charge or by their restricting employment to OD. The Monopolies Commission issued reports critical of the scale fees charged by estate agents, surveyors and architects, and recommended that advertising restrictions for accountants and solicitors be removed. The fees of civil engineers, medical practitioners, osteopaths, veterinary surgeons and stockbrokers have all been scrutinised. In the United States, it has been argued that restrictions on entry to medical schools and on recognition of foreign medical qualifications result in the highest medical fees in the world.[3]

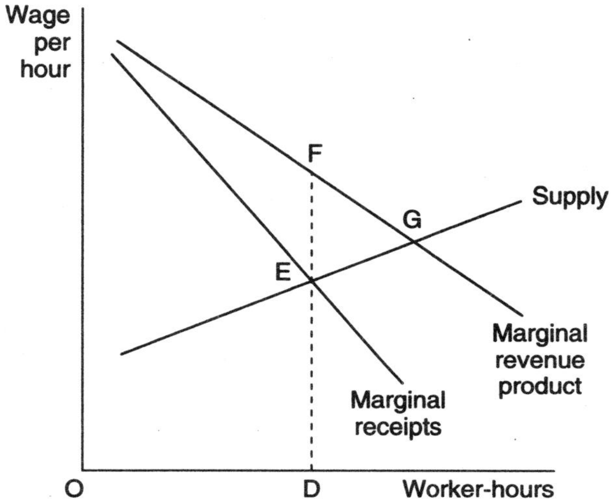

Figure 11.2 Monopoly in the labour market

Bilateral monopoly

These examples illustrate the separate occurrence of monopsony and monopoly in labour markets; but the two are most often to be found together. As J.K. Galbraith pointed out, power begets countervailing power, so that the monopsony power of mine-owners in isolated mining communities was matched by the unionisation of miners, the monopsony power of local authorities and central government matched by the growth of white-collar unions, and so on. When a monopsonist employer faces a monopolist supplier of services the resulting wage is indeterminate, lying between the monopsonist's favoured payment, AB in Figure 11.1, and the monopolist fee, DG of Figure 11.2. The outcome depends upon bargaining power.

Trade unions

Trade unions are usually thought of as bargainers on behalf of their members, although most of the time of local officials is taken up acting as a channel of communication between workers and managers, expressing and resolving grievances. Companies large enough to operate an internal market have often been among the supporters of post-entry closed shops because if all employees are members of a single union information travels to and fro with greater freedom. However, the role of unions as negotiators is the one that attracts attention.

Negotiating inevitably involves some posturing. Failure to agree, resulting in a strike, is likely to be costly for both employer and employee. The employer loses profits and the employee wages. A week's wages equals a 2 per cent increase in the wage rate so it is best not to hold out too long. As agreement is eventually reached, disagreement means a failure of one or both parties to recognise the true situation. The peculiarity of bargaining may be seen in the pay-off matrix of a bargaining game. In the simplest case each party may be accommodating or aggressive with pay-offs of the following orders of magnitude. The employer's pay-offs are given first.

		Trade Union	
		Accommodating	Aggressive
Employer	Accommodating	+10, +10	–20, +20
	Aggressive	+20, –20	–50, –50

If pay-offs follow this pattern, it is clearly against the interest of both parties to meet aggression with aggression, but each gains by making the other think he is determined to win the day. Hence the posturing, claims of solidarity and assertions that support is crumbling. Most breakdowns in negotiations occur because of inequalities of information, and proposals for improving labour relations turn on improving the knowledge of both sides.

5 SUMMARY

- Supplying labour means in the first place finding a job. Search continues so long as the gain in present value of prospective income exceeds the costs in time, money and income forgone.
- Job search helps explain frictional unemployment, the high rate of labour turnover of juveniles, and the range of wage payments in comparable occupations.

- Jobs are secured by successfully signalling the abilities on offer. Educational attainment is an important signal especially in the early part of a career.
- Signalling offers an alternative explanation to investment in human capital for the association of higher education with higher lifetime earnings.
- Large companies organise an internal labour market to provide for their needs beyond the initial recruitment level.
- Internal markets control the provision of specific training, provide for promotion, reconcile the interests of employer and employee, reduce the costs of monitoring and supervision, raise productivity and earnings, and reduce labour turnover.
- Monopsony in labour markets leads to wages being lower than marginal revenue products. A minimum wage imposed in such markets could lead to increased output and employment.
- Monopoly in labour markets has been found mainly in the liberal professions, where it is sometimes thought that maintaining standards involves restricting supply.
- Monopsony power begets monopoly power, and vice versa, so that bilateral monopoly is found more often than either monopsony or monopoly on its own. The outcome with bilateral monopoly depends upon the bargaining skill and power of the two sides.
- In bilateral negotiations over wages it is in the interests of each side to reach agreement, but not to be too agreeable whilst doing so.

Part V

CONCLUSION

12

APPROACHES TO GENERAL EQUILIBRIUM

1 INTRODUCTION

As more and more market links are traced between economic decisions, processes and products the prospect opens up that it may be possible to connect everything in a grand theory of general equilibrium. This prospect has attracted strictly practical economists who have developed input–output analysis, and pure theorists who have defined the conditions under which general equilibrium would be attained in a decentralised economy where decisions are taken independently in response to market signals and who have specified the features that would ensure economic efficiency in such an economy. It turns out that the pure theorists' constructions have important warnings for those who would rely on markets to secure full employment, growing output and efficient production and exchange.

The next three sections are devoted to input–output analysis: section 2 gives a short description of the analysis, section 3 applies it to the operation of sanctions against the white secessionist government of Southern Rhodesia (Zimbabwe), and section 4 examines some typical input–output patterns. Sections 5 and 6 are devoted to general equilibrium theory, looking first at the conditions for the existence of general equilibrium, and secondly, at theoretical and modified criteria for economic efficiency.

2 INPUT–OUTPUT ANALYSIS

Imagine a simple economy consisting of households that supply factor services – man-hours, machine-hours, acre-hours and so on – to industries A, B and C, and to the government. The economy is not isolated but exports and imports from the rest of the world. The industries use factor services together with imports to produce intermediate goods for each other, for exports, consumer goods for households and supplies for government agencies. The government uses manufactures, imports and factor services to provide goods for households. These flows of inputs and outputs may be set out in the matrix of an input–output table as in Table 12.1.

Reading down an industry column, the inputs used by each industry are shown. For example, Industry A obtains £13 million of its requirements from Industry B and £6 million from Industry C. It uses £3 million of imported goods. Finally, it obtains £51 of factor services as shown by the value added figure. Reading across a row, the figures show the destination of the output of an industry. For example, we have already seen that £13 million of the output of Industry B is sold to Industry A. In addition £18 million of B's output is sold to C, £65 million is exported, and £70 million sold to households and government. The table shows no entries for intra-industry transactions although firms within a single industry often supply one another with intermediate goods. This follows early practice: it avoids difficulties of estimating intra-industry transactions which may take place within integrated firms.

Analysis with constant proportions

An input–output table of itself is simply a description of transactions within an economy; but if we may assume that outputs vary in constant proportion with inputs, an input–output table may be used as a basis for analysing economic changes. If output always varies in constant proportion to input then £1 of output of Industry A would *directly* require £13/73-worth of output of B, £6/73 of output of C, £3/73 of imports, and £51/73 of factor services. These are the proportions shown in the column for Industry A.

The assumption that twice as much input produces twice as much output is reasonable as a first approximation in short-run analysis; but it is a restrictive assumption. It implies that there are no economies of scale, no possibilities of adapting methods of production to changes in factor prices, and no technological advances making possible reductions in input requirements. However, let us assume that production relationships are frozen in the proportions shown in the input–output table.

On this assumption the effects may be traced of changes in the

Table 12.1 A simple input–output table (£million)

Into:	*Industry A*	*Industry B*	*Industry C*	*Final demand*		*Gross output*
				Exports	*Households & Govt*	
From:						
Industry A	–	24	–	39	10	73
Industry B	13	–	18	65	70	166
Industry C	6	17	–	64	175	262
	19	41	18	168	255	
Imports	3	57	18	12	59	149
Value added	51	68	226			345
Gross outlay	73	166	262	180	314	

economy. Suppose, for instance, that there is an increase in household demand for products of Industry B. In order to increase output in B, output in Industries A and C must increase, and these increases have further repercussions. Increased output from A calls for additional supplies from Industries B and C, which means that B's output has to be increased further, implying further increases from A and C, implying . . . Similarly, increased output from Industry C calls for additional supplies from B, which involves increased output from C, and so on. A change in any part of the economy has repercussions throughout the entire economic system.

It would be possible to work out the repercussions using a step-by-step process tracing one adjustment after another, but it would call for a great deal of time and patience. Fortunately, the problem is a simple one in matrix algebra, and so input–output analysis is a practical method of forecasting the effects of economic changes. The power of this method may be seen from its application to forecasting the effects of Rhodesian sanctions.

3 INPUT–OUTPUT AND ZIMBABWE-RHODESIA

On 11 November 1965, the self-governing colony of Rhodesia declared itself independent in an effort to preserve its whites-dominated constitution. The response of the British government was to invite the United Nations to impose economic sanctions against Rhodesia. Sanctions took two forms: mandatory sanctions that required members of the UN to withhold supplies of oil from Rhodesia, and, secondly, a boycott by members of exports from Rhodesia so that Rhodesia would lack the means to pay for imports.

No informed observer expected mandatory oil sanctions to have any effect. South Africa did not accept the policy, and there was no provision for restricting supplies to South Africa. Rhodesia's total requirements for oil did not exceed 400,000 tons per year, roughly equal to the consumption of Greater Manchester, and this quantity could easily be supplied by rail and road. It was expected that the French company, Total, associated in joint projects with the South African government, would take over supply from British companies, and that British Petroleum and Shell would pick up some trade from Total elsewhere. This happened for a time, and the fact that subsidiaries of British companies eventually resumed supplying Rhodesia made no essential difference.

What about the effects of the boycott of Rhodesian exports? How would this work, and what size of effects might be expected?

Forecast I

In January 1966, Harold Wilson, then Prime Minister, expressed the opinion that 'the cumulative effects of economic sanctions might well bring the rebellion to an end in a matter of weeks rather than months'. This forecast had the saving grace that it could not mislead for long. It may have been based on the prospects threatened by the export multiplier: falling exports implying falling incomes for exporters who would be forced to spend less, leading to lower incomes for their suppliers who would be forced to spend less, and so on. This kind of analysis ignores the possibility that the Rhodesian government might increase expenditure to offset falling export receipts, and also, more importantly, it ignores the possibility of changing the work performed by Rhodesians.

Forecast II

In February 1967, T.R.C. Curtin and D. Murray completed a forecast of the effects of sanctions using input–output analysis which enabled them to take account of likely changes in the structure of the Rhodesian economy.[1] They began by observing that incomes of white Rhodesians were on average 25 per cent greater than those of white South Africans, and asked how far these incomes could fall before white Rhodesians would either eject the Rhodesian Front government or emigrate in such numbers that white supremacy would be untenable. This gave a bench-mark for evaluating effects. They decided that incomes of half the white population would have to fall by 25 per cent for sanctions to be effective. This implied a reduction in white incomes of £14 million, and, if total earnings maintained their proportion of National Income, a fall in National Income of £60 million, or 17 per cent.

Table 12.2 is a summary input–output table based on Curtin and Murray's much fuller estimates. It has a familiar look because it is simply Table 12.1 with Agriculture, Manufacturing and Other replacing Industries A, B and C. If the boycott of Rhodesian exports were implemented by all countries except South Africa, exports would fall by £100 million, and if the economy adjusted mechanically to such a fall, National Income and personal incomes would

Table 12.2 Input–output table for Rhodesia, 1964 (R£million)

Into:	*Agriculture*	*Manufacturing*	*Other*	*Final demand*		*Gross output*
				Exports	*Households & Govt*	
From:						
Agriculture	–	24	–	39	10	73
Manufacturing	13	–	18	65	70	166
Other	6	17	–	64	175	262
	19	41	18	168	255	
Imports	3	57	18	12	59	149
Value added	51	68	226			345
Gross outlay	73	166	262	180	314	

Source: Based upon fuller table in T.R.C. Curtin and D. Murray, *Economic sanctions and Rhodesia*, Institute of Economic Affairs, London, 1967, p. 36

fall by the requisite amounts. However, there is no reason to suppose such a mechanical response. About one-half of Rhodesian manufactures competed with imports, and these manufactures would be bound to expand if foreign competition were cut off. Indeed a trade boycott amounts to complete protection for domestic industries. When the repercussions of a projected fall in exports of £100 million together with an expansion of one-half of manufacturing industry are worked through the input–output matrix, the possible fall in National Income would not, according to Curtin and Murray, exceed 4 per cent. The two authors therefore forecast that sanctions would fail.

Outcome v. forecast

The actual outcome proved for a decade to be even more favourable to the white rebels. Manufacturing production fell by 5 per cent in 1966, but after that increased by 6–8 per cent annually for the next nine years. Real income per head rose by 6 per cent per year over the same period. After a small net emigration of white people after the declaration of independence, there was net white immigration until 1976. Events had turned out even more favourably for white Rhodesians than Curtin and Murray predicted. This was partly because exports fell by only two-thirds of the amount assumed for their calculations, but also because the adjustments were made in the structure of employment as they had forecast. After 1974 Rhodesian fortunes changed drastically. Manufacturing output began falling in 1975, real incomes slumped to the level of ten years earlier, and emigrants began to outnumber immigrants. This was Rhodesia's share of the world-wide slump caused by the high oil prices exacted by OPEC. Oil was eventually to be the Nemesis of white Rhodesians, but not for reasons envisaged when sanctions were introduced.

4 INPUT–OUTPUT PATTERNS

Rhodesia's ability to cope with economic sanctions stemmed partly from the limited development of the economy. This meant that interconnections between separate activities were much looser than in an advanced industrial economy. Tobacco growing, for example, felt the impact of sanctions more than most other activities with output at one stage falling by one-half; but this only involved 3,000 white farmers (together with very large numbers of black employees). Tobacco growing took few inputs from elsewhere in Rhodesia and its output went almost entirely to foreigners. Curtin and Murray made estimates of input and output for seven industrial sectors. There are thus forty-two cells in this part of their matrix but only seven show transactions amounting to 5 per cent of the output of the selling industry. Input–output tables for developing countries consist largely of blanks, the significance of such a table being what is not there.

The picture of a developed economy is very different. A 256 × 256 matrix for the British economy, for example, shows an intricate network of interdependence. A pattern may be discovered if the industries buying intermediate inputs but selling mainly to final demand appear in the top rows and left columns, and industries using basic factor services and selling mainly to other industries appear in the bottom rows and right columns. The transactions then form a right-angled triangle with its peak in the top left corner of the table. The triangulated table for Britain has industries such as clothing, furniture, food, drink and tobacco at the top left, and industries supplying basic services, such as electricity, communications and transport, at the bottom right. The triangulated tables for developed countries show a family resemblance to one another with the same industries to be found at peak and base. Input–output tables for developing countries do not triangulate.[2]

5 THE EXISTENCE OF GENERAL EQUILIBRIUM

Input–output matrices picture flows of transactions taking place between people and agencies making up an economy. Theorists have questioned whether such flows could ever become steady so that equilibrium obtained overall.

Counting equations

This possibility is properly the concern of mathematical economists, and in recent years of very high-powered ones; but it is possible to see where their investigations have led without getting deeply involved. It will be recalled from the simultaneous equations of school algebra that it took two equations, no more, no less, to determine two unknowns, three equations to determine three unknowns, and that is as far as elementary algebra usually goes. The principle, however, is quite general: to solve a set of simultaneous equations we need as many equations as unknowns. This was the approach adopted by Leon Walras to demonstrate the existence of general equilibrium.[3]

Consider an economy in which there is perfect competition in all markets, that is, households and firms make their decisions in terms of prices of goods and factor services given by the market, and, to shorten the argument, that there are fixed quantities of inputs available: *m* productive services to produce *n* products. In competitive conditions, the cost of production of each commodity must equal its price, and so there are *n* equations of the form:

$\text{input}_1 \times \text{factor price}_1 + \text{input}_2 \times \text{factor price}_2 + \ldots$
$+ \text{input}_m \times \text{factor price}_m = \text{price of product}_1$

In addition, equilibrium in the market for factor services requires that the total quantities of productive services offered must equal the total quantities supplied, so there are *m* equations of the form:

input_1 used in producing the first commodity + input_1 used in producing the second commodity + . . . + input_1 used in producing the *n*th commodity = quantity of input_1 supplied.

On the demand side, households maximise satisfaction by equating the marginal rate of substitution of commodity_1 for commodity_2 to the price of commodity_2 divided by the price of commodity_1, over all pairs of commodities so that there are $(n–1)$ such equations, the *n*th quantity being determined by the amount of income left after buying the $(n–1)$ items. Individual households are assumed to spend their entire income so that the sum of values of quantities bought must equal their receipts from sale of productive services. The *n* equations for households determine the quantities of various commodities bought. Bringing the *n* supply equations into equality with the *n* demand equations determines the *n* product prices. It is possible to elaborate this system of equations, but the nature of the argument does not change.

Unfortunately, counting equations and finding them sufficient to determine all quantities and prices does not prove that a general equilibrium exists. The mathematics might call for negative production or negative prices, and it is not always possible to attach economic meaning to such solutions of a system of simultaneous equations.

Modern proof of existence of general equilibrium

It has therefore been necessary to look more closely at the conditions that would ensure the attainment of a general equilibrium. In the 1950s Kenneth Arrow and Gerard Debreu showed that prices and quantities of all goods and services would reach equilibrium levels as a consequence of independent decisions by households and firms provided that there was perfect competition in all markets, with no significant economies of scale, no external costs or benefits, complete flexibility of wages and prices, and with a complete set of markets for 'dated, contingent commodities'.

The last requirement distinguishes the Arrow–Debreu model. They defined goods in terms of four attributes: physical characteristics, location, date of delivery, and the state of nature when delivered. For example, fuel oil of 0.92 specific gravity delivered New York on 7 January 1999, in the middle of a cold snap is a different good from fuel oil on the same day in New York in a mild spell. Arrow–Debreu require that all goods defined in this way have markets, and in doing so remove any complications arising from time or uncertainty. It can be proved that general equilibrium in an Arrow–Debreu economy would be economically efficient in the sense that it would be impossible to make anyone better off without making someone worse off.

Proof of the possibility of all plans of producers and consumers being reconciled in a world that has never existed nor is ever likely to exist may seem an odd accomplishment for two Nobel Prize winners; but two consequences of the proof deserve notice. First, there is no economic basis for political dogmas asserting that economic problems can be overcome by leaving everything to the operation of free markets, that excess demand in a market will be removed by rising price and increased supply and excess supply removed by falling price and reduced supply. This could happen; but it can only be proved to happen in the very artificial Arrow–Debreu conditions. Reality departs from these conditions in so many ways that the presumption must be that we are likely to experience general disequilibrium. If the disequilibrium is in labour markets the human cost can be serious: excess supply in such markets is a euphemism for unemployment. The Arrow–Debreu proof provides a presumption that government intervention is likely to be needed.

Secondly, the proof points towards the kinds of intervention likely to be needed. It provides theoretical underpinning for Keynesian employment policies, indicative planning for economic growth, and co-ordinated investment programmes such as those within Japanese industrial groups. All these policies are justified by the absence of markets for 'dated, contingent commodities', apart from limited insurance and futures markets. There is no *a priori* reason for expecting that expenditure plans for future production will exactly offset saving plans: hence Keynesian stabilisation policies. There is no reason why individual investment programmes will be compatible with the highest attainable rate of growth: hence indicative planning by firms and government agencies acting in co-operation to bring into being consistent programmes on mutually agreed assumptions about the future. There is no reason to suppose that individual firms acting independently will not build excess capacity: hence the interlocking shareholdings and involvement of banks in Japanese industrial groups. It must be remembered, of course, that government agents may be ill-informed, incompetent, privately motivated if not corrupt, and that administrative remedies may be worse than market mistakes.

6 WELFARE CONDITIONS

It was mentioned above that general equilibrium in an Arrow–Debreu world would be economically efficient in the sense that it would not be possible to make anyone better off without making someone worse off. There are many such equilibria, each corresponding to a different distribution of ownership of productive resources (including ability, education and training). Efficiency is attained because, with perfect competition in all markets, consumers and producers act as price-takers adjusting to the common set of prices given to them by impersonal market processes, and prices reflect all costs and benefits because there are no externalities. Efficiency in production, consumption, and the adjustment of production to consumers' wishes provide examples.

Efficient production

Consider two firms producing different goods, a staple and a luxury, with two inputs, labour and capital. If the marginal rates of substitution of labour for capital differ in the two firms it would be possible to increase production without increasing quantities of inputs simply by changing the disposition of factors between the two firms. For instance, if the marginal rate of substitution of labour for capital in staples is two, that is, two units of labour are needed to replace one unit of capital whilst maintaining output of staples constant, and the marginal rate of substitution of labour for capital in luxuries is three, that is, three units of labour are needed to replace one unit of capital in luxuries, then by transferring two units of labour from luxury production to staples it would be possible to release one unit of capital for luxuries, sufficient to replace three units of labour, and so one unit of labour would be spare and available for increased production. This possibility does not arise when each firm seeks least cost of production in terms of the same market-determined prices for labour and capital. Each adjusts its use of factors so that the marginal rate of substitution of labour for capital equals the ratio of the price of capital to the price of labour, and, as factor prices are the same for both firms, each must adjust so that marginal rates of substitution between factors are the same in each firm.

Efficient consumption

In like manner, it would not be possible to increase satisfaction of one consumer, except at the expense of another, because marginal rates of substitution between goods in consumption must be the same for all consumers. If they were not the same it would be possible to make one or both better off by changing the distribution of goods. For example, if one consumer regarded two units of staples equivalent to one unit of luxuries and another consumer regarded three units of staples equivalent to one unit of luxuries, then the latter could give up two units of staples for one unit of luxuries, leaving the first consumer no worse off and the second better off by one unit of staples. Such situations are ruled out by all consumers adjusting to given market prices. The adjustment brings marginal rates of substitution between goods into equality for all consumers.

Efficient relationship of production to consumption

A third source of inefficiency would be the possibility of substituting one good for another in production on different terms than they are substituted by householders in consumption; but, once more, the possibility is ruled out by firms and households adjusting to the same set of market prices. The marginal cost of staples is the cost of changing production of staples by one unit, and the marginal cost of luxuries is the cost of changing production of luxuries by one unit. Reducing production of staples by one unit would release resources worth the marginal cost of staples and these would enable production of luxuries to be increased by an amount equalling the marginal cost of staples divided by the marginal cost of luxuries: for example, if the marginal cost of staples is £1 and the marginal cost of luxuries £2, reducing production of staples by one unit makes possible production of one-half unit of luxuries. The marginal rate of transformation of staples into luxuries is therefore equal to the ratio of the marginal cost of staples to the marginal cost of luxuries.

In perfect competition profit maximisers operate rates of production at which marginal cost equals price. The marginal rate of transformation of staples into luxuries thus equals not only the ratio of marginal cost of staples to marginal cost of luxuries but also the ratio of the price of staples to the price of luxuries. Consumers adjust their choices so that the marginal rate of substitution of luxuries for staples equals the ratio of the price of staples to the price of luxuries. Hence the marginal rate of substitution of luxuries for staples in consumption equals the marginal rate of transformation of staples into luxuries in production. If it is possible to transform one unit of luxuries into two units of staples, and consumers regard two units of staples as equivalent to one unit of luxuries, then production and consumption have been brought into an efficient relationship: and this is all done by firms and households adjusting to market prices. As Adam Smith puts it, firms are led by an invisible hand to promote an end that is no part of their intention.

Implications

It is important not to be carried away by the welfare properties of a perfectly competitive general equilibrium. Remember that the particular equilibrium depends upon the particular distribution of resources, and that externalities, monopolies and complications of time and uncertainty have been assumed away. The welfare properties of an Arrow–Debreu world are therefore not found in reality.

It is tempting to suppose that economic efficiency could be improved in the real world by satisfying efficiency conditions as closely as possible. This is sometimes the case: for example, if fixed quantities of goods are to be rationed between consumers it will improve matters if this is done by rationing purchasing power rather than by allocating physical quantities. However, general equilibrium theory warns that the repercussions of adjusting production or consumption at one point may make matters worse at another. The implications of efficiency conditions lie in two other directions.

First, efficiency conditions are means of identifying opportunity costs and marginal benefits in simplified conditions and they point towards the opportunity costs that must be taken into account in the real world. Opportunity cost may consist of the value forgone by one consumer because another is enjoying a good, say urban road space. The general equilibrium model with its conditions for efficient consumption questions whether opportunity costs are being properly taken into account.

Secondly, the analysis suggests ways of adjusting to conditions such as monopoly. For example, the production and sale of oil conspicuously fails to satisfy the conditions of perfect competition. The opportunity cost of North Sea oil to the British economy is the export price obtainable by selling abroad. If oil is to be sold at monopoly levels it is not efficient to sell North Sea gas, all used in the home market, at marginal cost. This would lead to inefficient substitution of natural gas for oil.

7 SUMMARY

- An input–output table describes the factor services, intermediate goods and finished goods flowing forward per period of time, and shows the interdependence of industries.
- An input–output matrix is transformed from a description into an analytical tool when the assumption of constant proportions between inputs and outputs is acceptable.
- Input–output relationships resemble one another in economies at the same level of development. Tables for Western Europe and the USA triangulate in very similar ways. Tables for developing countries show them possessing semi-isolated industries lacking support from interconnected activities.
- It is not sufficient to construct a system with as many equations

as unknown prices and quantities in order to be sure that a general equilibrium exists because some equations may imply negative production or negative prices.

- Arrow and Debreu have shown that a general equilibrium exists in an economic model with perfect competition in all markets, no external costs and benefits, complete flexibility of wages and prices, and a complete set of markets for 'dated, contingent commodities'.
- The Arrow-Debreu model shows the flimsy basis of dogmatic beliefs in the performance of free markets, and indicates kinds of intervention that may be needed to make markets work effectively.
- The Arrow-Debreu model has properties that ensure economically efficient production, consumption, and relationship between production and consumption. These properties help to identify opportunity costs and point towards desirable price adjustments.

NOTES

1 THE ECONOMIC WAY OF THINKING

1 This example of the economic way of thinking is possibly too typical: it simplifies and possibly oversimplifies. For example, account should be taken of the fact that sales of new books depend upon display as well as price. Sales of new and second-hand books per foot of shelving need comparing along with the mark-up on each type of book. Again it is not difficult to think of other substitutes for new books in addition to second-hand books. Pubs surrounding LSE became more crowded as second-hand book sales expanded. Charing Cross Road with its second-hand bookshops is not far from LSE, and it might be argued that the second-hand trade was provided for before the Economist Bookshop became involved.

2 This example of cattle feeding, together with the later one on making ice-cream, is based on R.M. Morris, *Using linear models: formulation, optimisation and interpretation*, T341 3/4, Milton Keynes, Open University, 1975.

3 This argument obviously ignores the benefit of longer courses. It is not clear that the shortness of British courses compared with European, American and Japanese is a cause for pride.

4 I am indebted to Lt Cmdr Harry Watters RNVR, Flotilla Officer, 326 Rocket Flotilla, for the explanation of ship-handling.

2 FIRMS, MARKETS AND INDUSTRIES

1 As will be seen in Chapter 7, the sales of individual firms may be highly elastic for price increases, and less elastic for price reductions, because of the reactions of rivals. Here we are concerned with the responsiveness of sales if all established suppliers should raise their prices.

2 The late Mr W. Wragg of Sheffield took some satisfaction from finding that he met the monopoly criteria precisely. He was the sole British manufacturer of tuning forks, sheltered by a protective tariff. The price elasticity and cross-elasticities of demand were low because the

only close substitute for a tuning fork was another tuning fork. He was aware of five other manufacturers in the world but made no conjectures about their prices beyond making sure that his prices never exceeded the tariff differential. The barrier to entry was high because Mr Wragg employed the only metal-worker skilled in tuning by ear, and because he was equipped with an electronic counter installed by the government for war work. Mr Wragg is instructive in three respects: first, the strongest source of monopoly power in the past was tariff protection and the strongest corrosive to such power is provided by free trade; secondly, monopolies are likely to abound in niche markets that provide exclusive but strictly limited opportunities; and thirdly, monopolies are vulnerable to technological progress. Tuning forks are still used for tuning pianos, but they no longer feature in bomb sights and very few doctors make diagnoses with them.

3 J. Robinson, *Contributions to modern economics*, Oxford, Basil Blackwell, 1978, p. 167.

3 AIMS OF BUSINESS

1 T. Scitovsky, 'A note on profit maximisation and its implications', *Review of Economic Studies*, Vol. XI, 1943, pp. 57–60, reprinted in K.E. Boulding and G.J. Stigler (eds), *Readings in price theory*, London, Allen & Unwin, 1953, pp. 352–8.

2 S. Nyman and A. Silberston, 'The ownership and control of industry', in A.P. Jacquemin and H.W. de Jong (eds), *Welfare aspects of industrial markets*, Leiden, Martinus Nijhoff, 1977, pp. 43–69. This chapter critically reviews the main investigations of the divorce of ownership from control and summarises the authors' own important research in this area.

3 R. Marris, 'A model of the "managerial" enterprise', *Quarterly Journal of Economics*, Vol. LXXVII, 1963, pp. 185–209. See also H. Radice, 'Control type, profitability and growth in large firms: an empirical study', *Economic Journal*, Vol. 81, 1971, pp. 547–62.

4 W.J. Baumol, *Business behavior, value and growth*, Macmillan, New York, 1959, chaps 6–8, pp. 45–82.

5 O.E. Williamson, *Economic organisation: firms, markets and policy control*, Brighton, Wheatsheaf, 1986, chap. 2, pp. 6–31.

6 H.A. Simon, 'Theories of decision-making in economics and behavioural science', in American Economic Association and Royal Economic Society, *Surveys of economic theory*, Vol. III, London, Macmillan, 1966, pp. 1–28.

4 THREE MEANINGS OF COMPETITION

1 Evidence of competitive activity in pharmaceuticals is taken from National Economic Development Office, *Focus on pharmaceuticals*, London, HMSO, 1972.

2 P.T. Bauer and B.S. Yamey, *Markets, market control and marketing reform*, London, Weidenfeld & Nicolson, 1968, chap. 4, pp. 69–81.

3 D.R. Oldroyd, *Darwinian impacts*, Milton Keynes, Open University, 1980, p. 216.

4 Armen Alchian's comment is apposite: 'It might, however, be argued that the facts of life deny even a substantial role to the element of chance and the associated adoption principle in the economic system. For example, the long lives and disparate sizes of business firms and hereditary fortunes may seem to be reliable evidence of consistent foresighted motivation and non-random behaviour. In order to demonstrate that consistent success cannot be treated as prima facie evidence against pure luck, the following chance model of Borel, the famous French mathematician is presented.

'Suppose two million Parisians were paired off and set to tossing coins in a game of matching. Each player plays until the winner of the first toss is again brought to equality with the other player. Assuming one toss per second for each eight-hour day, at the end of ten years there would still be, on the average, about a hundred-odd pairs; and if the players assign the game to their heirs, a dozen or so will still be playing at the end of a thousand years! The implications are obvious. Suppose that some business has been operating for one hundred years. Should one rule out luck and chance as the essence of the factors producing the long-term survival of the enterprise? No inference whatever can be drawn until the number of original participants is known; and even then one must know the size, risk and frequency of each commitment. One can see from the Borel illustration the danger in concluding that there are too many firms with long lives in the real world to admit an important role to chance. On the contrary, one might insist that there are actually too few!' (A.A. Alchian, *Economic forces at work*, Indianapolis, Liberty Press, 1977, pp. 23–4.

5 Far from it: it is unfortunately the case that in large cities the provision of the services of the oldest profession fits the purely competitive model. See R. Fels, 'The price of sin', in R. Fels and R.G. Uhler, *Casebook of economic problems and policies*, St Paul, West, 1974, reprinted in H.Townsend (ed.), *Price theory*, 2nd edn, Harmondsworth, Penguin Books, 1980, pp. 302–3.

6 This was the assumption introduced by J.S. Bain in his influential *Barriers to new competition*, Cambridge, Mass., Harvard University Press, 1956.

7 Elizabeth Brunner, 'Industrial analysis revisited', in P.W.S. Andrews and E. Brunner, *Studies in Pricing*, London, Macmillan, 1975, p. 39: the chapter including this quotation is reprinted in Townsend, *Price theory*.

8 W. Baumol, 'Contestable markets: an uprising in the theory of industry structure', *American Economic Review*, Vol. LXXII, 1982, pp. 1–15.

5 PURE COMPETITION, PERFECT COMPETITION AND EFFICIENT MARKETS

1 E.H. Chamberlin gained widespread support for his large group case of monopolistic competition, which differed from pure competition in that each supplier differentiated his product by design, marketing or location. This seems to impart greater realism, and models can be developed in which equilibrium in an individual firm is characterised by tangency of a downward-sloping individual demand curve with the falling section of a long-run average cost curve. If the differences between products are meretricious, it may be argued that product differentiation leads to a market being supplied by too many firms operating on too small a scale. However, it is difficult to find cases where differentiation of products makes much difference to the outcome when there are large numbers of competitors. When there are large numbers of heterogeneous products within one market, the differences between them can only be minor, and the elasticity of demand facing individual firms must be very large although not infinite. Furthermore, economies of scale must be unimportant when there are large numbers of suppliers so that long-run average costs are unlikely to fall steeply. Although Chamberlin was an insistent advocate of monopolistic competition, his main contribution was in developing models of oligopoly with joint profit maximisation.

2 *Report of the committee on the taxicab service* (Runciman Report), Cmd 8804, London, HMSO, 1953; *The London taxicab trade* (Stamp Committee), Cmnd 4483, London, HMSO, 1970.

3 Purchase tax was imposed in the first place because private motorists were buying taxicabs to avoid purchase tax on private cars.

4 Runciman Report, Appendix V.

5 J.A. Dowie, 'Markets in risk', in Block 2, 'The world of monetary risk' of *Risk: a second level University course*, Milton Keynes, The Open University, 1980, pp. 100–1. See also J.A. Dowie, 'On the efficiency and equity of betting markets', *Economica*, Vol. 43, 1976, pp. 139–50.

6 M.G. Kendall, 'The analysis of economic time series, Part 1: Prices', *Journal of the Royal Statistical Society*, Vol. 96, 1953, pp. 11–25. Sir Maurice analysed nineteen series of share prices and three of commodity prices over long runs of years. L. Bachelier, in 1900, not only demonstrated the random walk of commodity prices but developed the mathematical theory of Brownian motion to describe the phenomena five years before Albert Einstein independently developed the same mathematics. L. Bachelier, *Théorie de la speculation*, Paris, Gauthier-Villars, 1900, translated into English by A.J. Boness in P.H. Cootner (ed.), *The random character of stock market prices*, Cambridge, Mass., MIT Press, 1964, pp. 17–78.

7 Consumers' Association, *Money Which?*, June 1974. Similar conclusions have been reached in subsequent surveys.

6 MONOPOLY AND ECONOMIC WELFARE

1 This is most easily proved by a few lines of calculus. It depends upon the relationship of price (average revenue) and marginal revenue: at the profit-maximising output marginal cost equals marginal receipts and so may be substituted for marginal receipts. The following geometrical proof, using Figure n.6.1, has the advantage of being visual. DM is a linear demand curve and DG the corresponding marginal revenue curve.

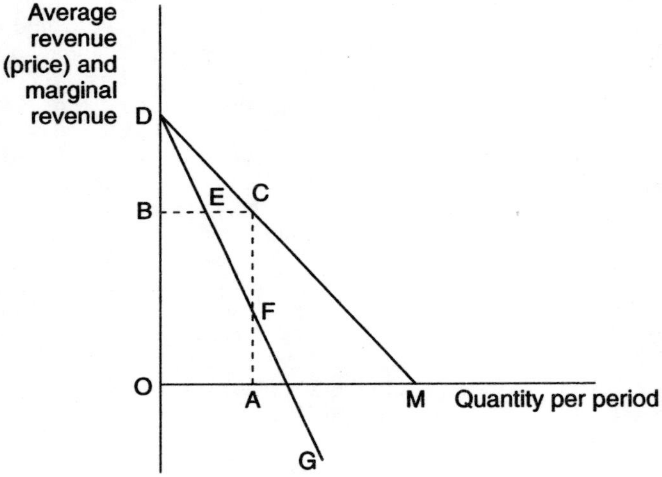

Figure n6.1 Geometry of average and marginal revenue

Total revenue, at price OB, equals OBCA (average revenue × quantity demanded) and also ODEFA (the sum of marginal revenues from successive units demanded). Therefore OBCA = ODEFA. These two areas have OBEFA in common. The two triangles BDE and ECF thus have equal areas and, as their angles are equal, are congruent triangles: BD = CF = AC – AF, that is, average receipts minus marginal receipts.

Price elasticity at C = MC/CD = OB/BD = OB/CF, i.e price divided by price minus marginal revenue. When marginal cost equals marginal revenue:

$$\text{Price elasticity} = \frac{\text{price}}{\text{price} - \text{marginal cost}}$$

that is, the reciprocal of the Lerner Index. Notice also that the elasticity relationship implies:

$$\text{price} = \text{marginal revenue} \times \frac{\text{elasticity}}{(\text{elasticity} - 1)}$$

This is used at the end of Chapter 7. The measurement of monopoly power is discussed at length in P. Asch, *Economic theory and the antitrust dilemma*, New York, John Wiley, 1970, pp. 133–66.

2 Monopolies and Mergers Commission, *Building bricks*, HC 474, 1975–6, *Plasterboard*, HC 94, 1973–4, *Flat glass*, HC 83, 1967–8, *Metal containers*, HC 6, 1970; London, HMSO.

3 OPEC's members are Saudi Arabia, Iran, Kuwait, Iraq, United Arab Emirates, Qatar, Libya, Algeria, Nigeria, Gabon, Ecuador, Venezuela and Indonesia. The individual roles of these countries within the cartel are considered in Chapter 7.

4 This estimate of the cost of OPEC ignores the diversion of resources into oil production outside the cartel. In a rational world it would not make sense to use $6 of resources to produce a barrel of oil in the North Sea when it could be obtained for 30 cents in Saudi Arabia.

5 An accurate estimate would call for an income-compensated demand curve which took account of the reduced purchasing power available for all purchases resulting from outlay on successive units. Income-compensated demand curves for normal goods lie to the left of conventional demand curves.

6 See S.L. Brue and D.R. Wentworth, *Economic scenes: theory in today's world*, 2nd edn, Englewood Cliffs, N.J., Prentice-Hall, 1980, pp. 111–14.

7 Authors being interested in total revenue wish to see price reduced so long as there is some consequent increase in revenue, that is, so long as marginal receipts are positive. At the author's ideal price marginal revenue is zero. This is less than ideal for the publisher facing positive marginal costs.

7 OLIGOPOLY: INTERDEPENDENT DECISIONS

1 Von Neumann and Morgenstern drew attention to the relevance of Sherlock Holmes in J. von Neumann and O. Morgenstern, *Theory of games and economic behaviour*, 3rd edn, New York, John Wiley, 1953, p. 177.

2 See D.W. Carlton, 'The theory and the facts of how markets clear', in R. Schmalensee and R.D. Willig (eds.), *Handbook of industrial organisation*, North-Holland, Elsevier, 1989, pp. 916–24.

3 H. Tucker invented the prisoners' dilemma game telling the fable of the Grand Vizier who has captured two villains but is unable to prove their guilt. He interviews them separately and offers the following terms: 'If you do not confess and your partner in crime confesses, he shall go free and you will hang. If you confess and your partner refuses to acknowledge his guilt, he shall hang and you will go free. If you both confess, you will both go to jail for ten years. If neither of you confesses, I shall be unable to keep you imprisoned for more than one year.' Both confess.

4 See R. Axelrod, *The evolution of cooperation*, New York, Basic Books, 1984.
5 Adam Smith, *Wealth of Nations*, ed. Cannan, London, Methuen, 1950, vol. I, bk 1, p. 130. Smith's praise of the invisible hand directing private profit-seeking towards public good is to be found in ibid., bk 4, p. 421.
6 Monopolies Commission, *Breakfast cereals*, HC 2, London, HMSO, 1973, para. 79.
7 Quoted in J. Backman, *Pricing: policies and practices*, New York, National Industrial Conference Board, 1961.
8 E. Kefauver, *In a few hands*, Harmondsworth, Penguin, 1966, pp. 143–50.
9 Monopolies and Mergers Commission, *White salt*, Cmnd 9778, London, HMSO, 1986, p. 86.
10 Quoted by W. Adams, 'The steel industry', in W. Adams (ed.), *The structure of American industry*, 5th edn, New York, Macmillan, 1977, p. 87.
11 J.A. Schumpeter, *Capitalism, socialism and democracy*, 2nd edn, New York, Harper, 1943, pp. 79ff.; J.K. Galbraith, *American capitalism*, London, Hamish Hamilton, 1952, chap. 7.
12 OPEC's members are Saudi Arabia, Iran, Kuwait, Iraq, United Arab Emirates, Qatar, Libya, Algeria, Nigeria, Gabon, Ecuador, Venezuela and Indonesia. Production figures are from *Petroleum Economist*.
13 The theory of cost-plus pricing where potential competition is strong was developed by P.W.S. Andrews. His best exposition is not very accessible, but well worth pursuing. See P.W.S. Andrews, 'Competition in the modern economy', in G. Sell (ed.), *Competitive aspects of oil operations*, London, Institute of Petroleum, 1958.

8 MARKET PROBLEMS: INFORMATION, EXTERNALITIES AND PROPERTY RIGHTS

1 G.A. Akerlof, 'The market for "lemons": qualitative uncertainty and the market mechanism', *Quarterly Journal of Economics*, Vol. LXXXIV, 1970, pp. 488–500.
2 L. Benham, 'The effect of advertising on the price of eyeglasses', *Journal of Law and Economics*, Vol. XV, 1972, pp. 337–52.
3 R.D. Feldman and J.W. Begun, 'Does advertising reduce the mean and variance of prices?', *Economic Inquiry*, Vol. XVIII, 1980, pp. 487–92.
4 H. Townsend, 'Economics of consumerism', *University of Lancaster Inaugural Lectures, 1973*.
5 J.K. Galbraith, *The affluent society*, Boston, Houghton Mifflin, 1958, pp. 121–2 and 120.
6 J. Best and T. Broadbent, 'The "Big John" campaign: advertising in the beer market', in S. Broadbent (ed.), *Advertising works 2*, London, Holt, Rinehart and Winston, 1983. The authors comment: 'Beer drinking is essentially social and group pressures can be strong. The public selection of a brand of beer reflects the buyer's self-image in the same way as choice of cigarettes, clothes or car. Buyers want to feel that

they are making a sensible, defensible choice that reflects well upon them as knowledgeable beer drinkers. This can override actual taste preference; the brewery adage that "people drink with their eyes" has been repeatedly confirmed by blind and branded product tests, where the brand-names can reverse the preferences expressed "blind".

'The under-30s tend not to be beer experts: they are too young. Their drinking is more influenced by what is popular and fashionable among their peer group.'

7 S.F. Witt and C.L. Pass, 'The effects of health warnings and advertising on the demand for cigarettes', *Scottish Journal of Political Economy*, Vol. 28, 1981, pp. 86–92. The estimates of Witt and Pass are made on a per head basis to standardise for population. Their estimate of 0.07 is relevant to commercial calculations. So far as health is concerned it must be remembered that most smokers are addicted, and so any increase in cigarette sales must come from new smokers, mainly young people. These make up possibly one-twentieth of the market, and so the advertising elasticity of demand for new smokers must be about $0.07 \times 20 = 1.4$.

8 K. Cowling, 'Optimality in firms' advertising policies: an empirical analysis', in K. Cowling (ed.), *Market structure and corporate behaviour*, London, Gray-Mills, 1972.

9 R. Dorfman and P.O. Steiner, 'Optimal advertising and optimal quality', *American Economic Review*, Vol. XLIV, 1954, pp. 826–36.

10 This improvement is often attributed to the Clean Air Act, 1956. The Act made a contribution, but the fall in air pollution followed the trend already established before 1956 as demand for oil and gas responded to relative prices and rising incomes.

11 Externalities may also escape the calculations of central planners. The horror stories coming out of Russia and Eastern Europe bear stark witness.

12 R.H. Coase, 'The problem of social cost', *Journal of Law and Economics*, Vol. 3, 1960, pp. 1–44.

9 MARGINAL PRODUCTIVITY AND FACTOR DEMAND

1 This description of the relationship of rates of input per period to rates of output per period has some implicit effects incorporated that should not be ignored. The maximum output a combination of inputs can produce depends upon sufficient time having been taken to plan the operation, and the maximum output may only be attainable after sufficient repetitions of production to allow for full learning by doing. It might be preferred to deal with these two considerations explicitly by making production a function of the timing of production, and a function of the cumulated amount of production, as well as of rates of input. See A. Alchian, 'Costs and outputs', in *The allocation of economic resources, essays in honor of B.F. Haley*, Stanford, Calif., Stanford University Press, 1959, pp. 23–40, reprinted in A. Alchian, *Economic forces at work*, Indianapolis, Liberty Press, 1977, pp. 273–300.

2 This is cavalier treatment of the extensive analysis of the incidence of company taxes which should properly be taken into account.

10 SUPPLY, SUPPLY AND DEMAND, AND RESTRICTED COMPETITION

1 See Central Statistical Office, *Social Trends 24*, London, HMSO, 1994, chap. 4.
2 See C.V. Brown, *Taxation and the incentive to work*, London, Oxford University Press.
3 The largest number of estimates of labour supply curves relate to the United States. These are surveyed in B.E. Kaufman, *The economics of labor markets and labor relations*, Chicago, Dryden Press, 1986, chaps 2–3.
4 Adam Smith, *Wealth of Nations*, ed. Cannan, London, Methuen, 1950, vol. I, bk 1, p. 101.
5 J. Gabriel, *Unqualified success*, Harmondsworth, Penguin, 1986, provides a comprehensive guide to the pros and cons of different jobs.
6 Population movements are sometimes seen as inexorable secular trends. It is worth remembering that if half the men and women aged 16 to 36 died in a single year and if the surviving pairs all had children in each successive year, population would recover to its original size in two years.
7 M.M. Postan, 'Some economic evidence of declining population in the later Middle Ages', *Economic History Review*, 2nd ser., II, 1950; reprinted in M.M. Postan, *Essays on mediaeval agriculture and general problems of the mediaeval economy*, Cambridge, Cambridge University Press, 1973, chap. 10.
8 See H. Phelps Brown and S.V. Hopkins, *A perspective on wages and prices*, London, Methuen, 1981.
9 See J. Hatcher, *Plague, population and the English economy 1348–1530*, London, Macmillan, 1977, p. 71.

11 MARKET COMPLICATIONS: INFORMATION, CO-OPERATION AND CONFLICT

1 See J.A. Paulos, *Innumeracy*, Penguin Books, London, 1988, pp. 37–9. Paulos examines a similar problem of sequential search, that of a young woman reviewing prospective partners, and explains that the 37 per cent rule is derived from the idea of conditional probability and a little calculus. He returns to the problem of sequential search in *Beyond numeracy*, Viking, London, 1991, p. 64, where he explains that if sequential search involves N candidates, some number K<N should be chosen and the first K candidates be rejected. The optimum K is (N × 1/e). 1/e is approximately 0.37. Hence the 37 per cent rule which gives a 37 per cent chance of finding the best candidate.
2 See D. Sapsford and Z. Tzannatos, *The economics of the labour market*, Macmillan, London, 1993, chap. 4.

3 Monopolies and Mergers Commission reports, 1975–8 and 1987.

12 APPROACHES TO GENERAL EQUILIBRIUM

1 T.R.C. Curtin and D. Murray, *Economic sanctions and Rhodesia*, IEA Research Monograph 12, London, Institute of Economic Affairs, 1967.
2 See W. Leontief, 'The structure of development', in W. Leontief, *Input–output economics*, 2nd edn, New York, Oxford University Press, 1986, chap. 8.
3 Gustav Cassel provides an easy approach to Walras's analysis. See G. Cassel, *The theory of social economy*, translated by S.L. Barron, London, Ernest Benn, 1932, pp. 137–64.

INDEX